SATYAGRAHA

THE STORY BEHIND THE REVOLUTION

Compiled & Edited by

Pooja Varma

Om Books International

Published in 2013 by

Om Books International in association with

Prakash Jha Productions

Corporate & Editorial Office
A-12, Sector 64, Noida 201 301
Uttar Pradesh, India
Phone: +91 120 477 4100
Email: editorial@ombooks.com
Website: www.ombooksinternational.com

Sales Office
4379/4B, Prakash House, Ansari Road
Darya Ganj, New Delhi 110 002, India
Phone: +91 11 2326 3363, 2326 5303
Fax: +91 11 2327 8091
Email: sales@ombooks.com
Website: www.ombooks.com

201-A&B, Abhishek, Off New Link Road
Andheri (West), Mumbai - 400 053, INDIA
Tel: + 91 22 66781862 Fax: +91 22 66781863
E-mail: info@prakashjhaproductions.com
www.prakashjhaproductions.com

Compiled & Edited
Pooja Varma

Design
Mayur Varma

Artwork
Studio Link Pvt. Ltd.

ISBN: 978-93-83202-73-7

Printed in India by Ajanta Offset & Packagings Ltd., New Delhi

10 9 8 7 6 5 4 3 2 1

To everyone who made it possible
for me to make this film…

Prakash Jha

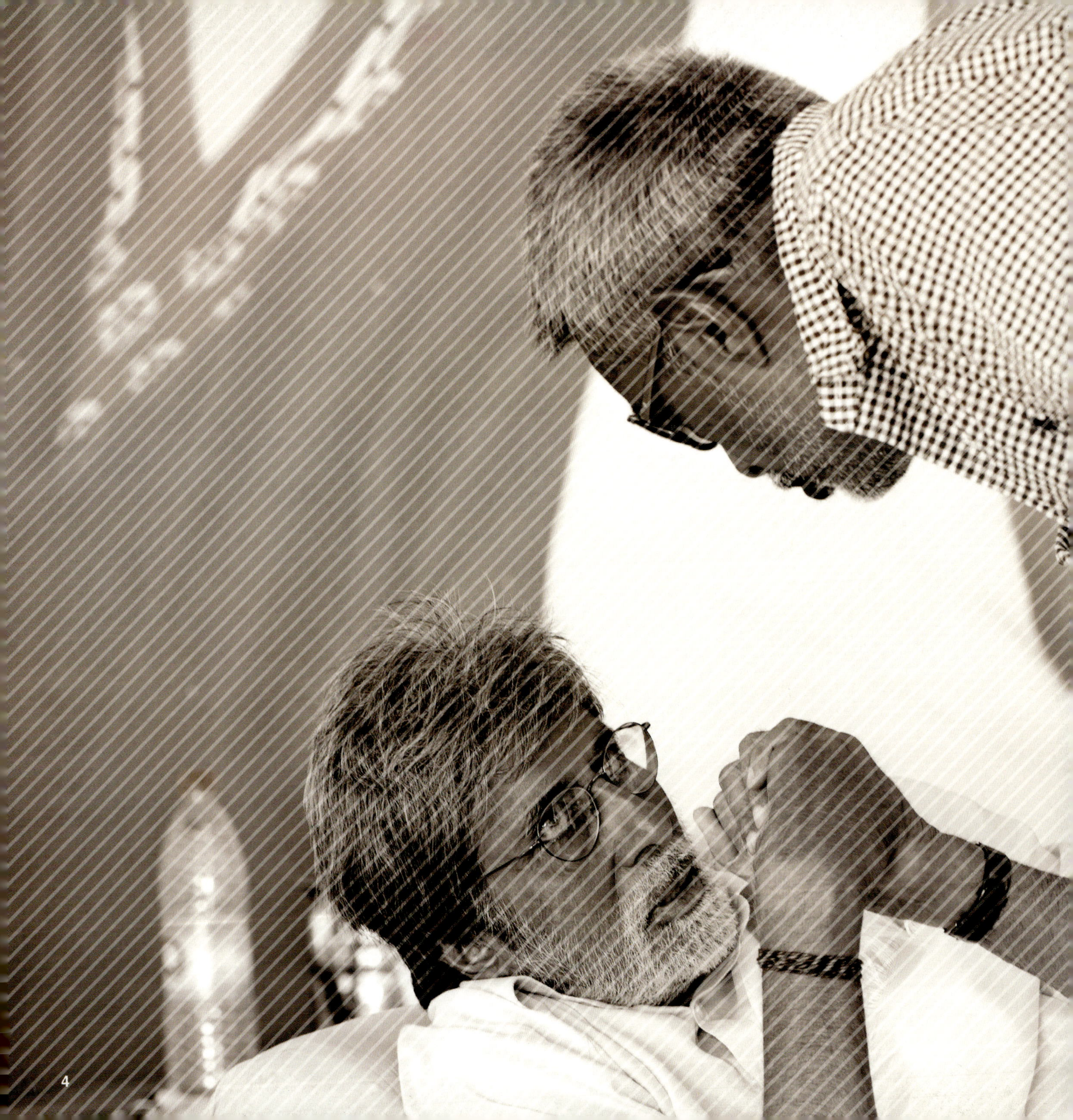

Contents

Prakash Jha

The middle class suddenly seems to have discovered its own power! Almost simultaneously, all over the world there seems to be an upsurge of protests and movements. Arab Spring... Wall Street... India! The India Against Corruption Movement was an astounding revelation of the public sentiment. And the sheer numbers in which crowds turned up for the unfortunate girl in Delhi!

Anjum Rajabali

People everywhere are finding themselves distressed as a result of the failure of governance. **Governments, even those democratically elected, can no longer be trusted to reflect the will of the people.** The only alternative, then, is for the people to express it themselves, in large enough numbers to make their governments hesitate before pursuing their violent agenda.

Prakash Jha It cannot be a coincidence that this is happening everywhere at the same time! I think there is a social pattern at play.

Anjum Rajabali

This fiery rage that has built up in the crowd has the power to change the future of our country if channelised well. The rage cannot be wasted on ego tussles with the government...

Anjum Rajabali shared an album **FIGHT for RIGHT**

Anjum Rajabali

Had a volatile (as usual) and invigorating (again, as usual) argument with Prakash Jha on the trend of protests breaking out everywhere. After an exciting shouting match, we have both agreed(!!) that it's because there has been a sea change in the attitude of the people towards their governments.

Prakash Jha I'm shocked too that we finally agreed on something!

Anjum Rajabali Yes! I think you need to start drinking again! Our arguments are not half as fun with you guzzling apple juice!

Prakash Jha Even if you got me drunk, you would still not be able to resist my 'market argument'!

Anjum Rajabali Ah yes! The 'market'! That has become more powerful than the government thanks to economic boom and liberalisation.

Prakash Jha Tell me about it! It created a massive number of job opportunities. And it has taught us Indians to get off our behinds and become performance oriented!

Anjum Rajabali And those who perform expect the same from others. You of all people should know that, the taskmaster that you are! :P

Prakash Jha Proudly so! :P

Prakash Jha But seriously, isn't it exciting? The new generation, the 'young India' does not recognise government supremacy as the final authority! They look at the government as a service provider to whom they pay tax. Sarkaar is no longer 'maai-baap'!

FREE
ADUJI
Prakash Jha
@prakash_jha1
Sarkaar is no longer maai-baap!
#NeverTrust a politician who asks you to sacrifice freedom.
Retweeted by Prakash Jha

Anjum Rajabali ▸ Prakash Jha

Have been thinking about our little 'friendly debate' the other night! There is another side to this change in attitude of the young India. This entire generation has changed the social map of our country. They have managed astounding material gains and professional achievements. And largely without having to be involved in the political framework of the country. It might sound a bit unbelievable, but I think **this entire generation has become depoliticised!**

Prakash Jha Hmm.. this is getting worrisome...I am finding myself agreeing with you again! I remember when we were studying, growing up, looking for career options – there were none! Except to join the IAS, or IPS or get some position in the government machinery. It was the only real achievement in those days. But today a government job is the last option for kids!

Anjum Rajabali It's like a sugar rush, their achievements. The younger generation started to feel like that they can almost do away with the politics, keep it at bay and continue to grow individually and as a country!

Prakash Jha But that's unrealistic, isn't it? It's like shutting your eyes and saying, 'it's dark'! No country can function for too long without a sound political direction.

Anjum Rajabali Yes! And now that they realise that, they're coming on to the streets! To change things. I think this could lead us somewhere. Are you thinking what I'm thinking?

Prakash Jha You can bet I am!

SrBachchan Looks like something is cooking, Mr. Jha, Anjum?!

👍 2

Prakash Jha :) Sir, you'll be the first one to be invited, when it's ready to serve!

👍 2

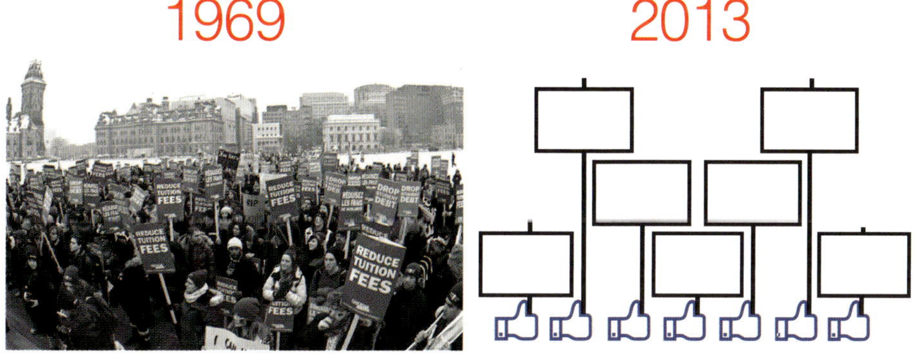

Comments:

Prakash Jha

Social media is the new medium of movements.

Prakash Jha has just read an article.

Nav Bharat post

Protesting peacefully is a science.

Read more

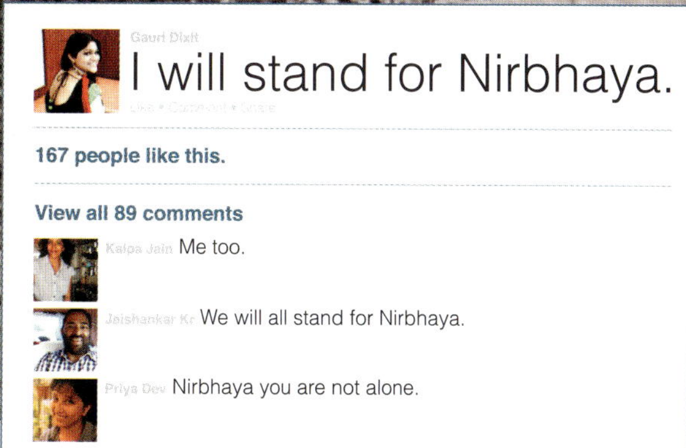

Aware India

The crowds refuse to budge from India Gate till the Anti Corruption Bill is passed.

321 people like this.

Lara Singh Roy

Reading a revolution! **- at Taksim Square, Turkey, Istanbul**

Anjum Rajabali ▸ Prakash Jha

Issues concerning an entire community are fought for in a mass protest. But if you look closely, it always begins as the pain and anguish of one person.

Prakash Jha When one man's anguish is felt by an entire people, it becomes a protest movement.

Anjum Rajabali I think we have a story.

1 Ronnie Screwvala likes this.

Ronnie Screwvala

I think we have a film.

Prakash Jha, Anjum Rajabali, SrBachchan like this.

Prakash Jha

Started work on the new one.

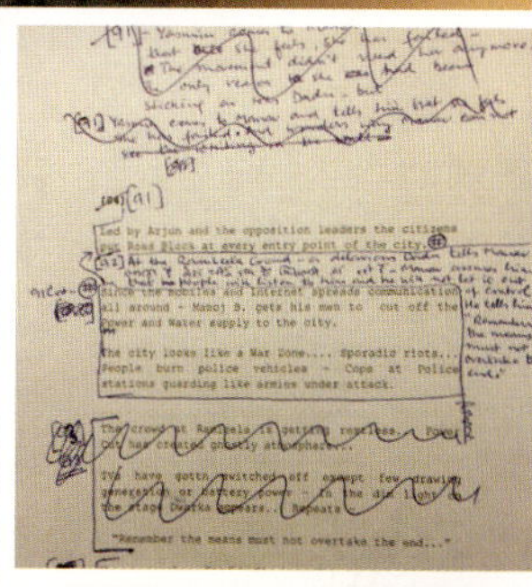

Led by Arjun and the opposition leaders the citizens
put Road Block at every entry point of the city.

Since the mobiles and Internet spreads communication
all around - Manoj B. gets his men to cut off the
Power and Water supply to the city.

The city looks like a War Zone.... Sporadic riots...
People burn police vehicles - Cops at Police
stations guarding like armies under attack.

"Remember the means must not overtake the end..."

Bangkok, September 2011. Paris, October 2011. Patna, February 2012

Satyagraha, the story of India's struggle - written all over the world!

Prakash Jha
@prakash_jha1
Our new film is the story of a movement sparked off by a personal tragedy. A movement that brings together millions of people to fight the demons of corruption. Title suggestions please? #PJPNewFilmTitle
Karan Talwar
@KaranTalwar
Sir, let's call it AAWAAZ... #PJPNewFilmTitle
Anshuman Gaitonde
@AnshuG
How about Inqilaab? #PJPNewFilmTitle
Iqbal Malik
@IqbalMalik
Satyamev Jayete #PJPNewFilmTitle
Sudhirbhai Misra
@SDBMisra
Meri Aawaz Suno #PJPNewFilmTitle
Harish Jain
@HJain
Bheed Bhadakka Mein Dhakka! #PJPNewFilmTitle
Iti Agarwal
@ItiAgarwalWrites
We the people take over! #PJPNewFilmTitle
Rehaan Mistry
@RehaanMystery
Sach ka sanghursh #PJPNewFilmTitle
Ketaki Roy
@MeKetakiRoy
Janta ka Judgement #PJPNewFilmTitle
Prakash Jha
@PrakashJha
Thank you for your suggestions #PJPNewFilmTitle

Chat between Prakash Jha, Anjum Rajabali
Prakash Jha
It should reflect what is happening, what shouldn't happen and what should happen in the country.
Anjum Rajabali
It all begins as a personal struggle. And the man behind the struggle seems to have a quiet strength about him. People back him up. And without anyone having planned it that way, the personal struggle escalates into a movement led by a seemingly harmless old man.
Prakash Jha
Anjum! I've got the title of the film! Why didn't I think of it before!
Anjum Rajabali
What's it?
Prakash Jha has left the chat
Anjum Rajabali
Prakash?
Are you there?
?

COMPANY
DAY-TO-DAY FLEXIBLE

Prakash Jha changed his cover photo.

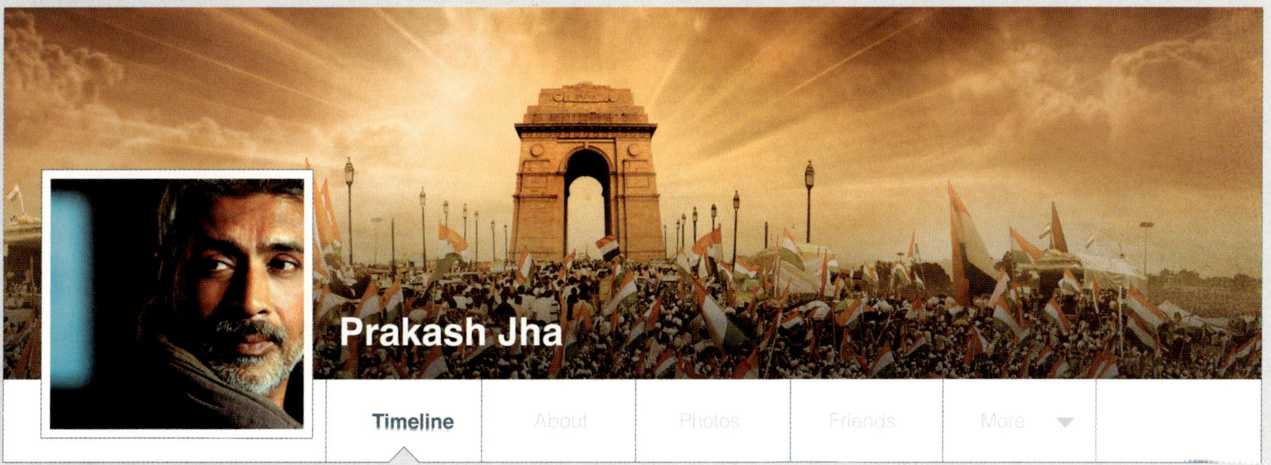

Prakash Jha posted a picture on his wall

Borrowing from the man who truly taught us to fight for truth!

Anjum Rajabali likes this.

Karan Talwar Associate Director posted

First day of shoot went smoothly. Off to a good start. The satyagrahi crowd artistes sat on the highway with such convincing determination that everyone passing by thought there was a real dharna and something was wrong! Some of them even considered turning back till we assured them that a camera was rolling and these were actors!

Prakash Jha The news of the 'dharna' reached Bhopal city too! A fellow guest at the hotel was helpfully advising me not to shoot for a few days, because there might be some kind of unrest caused by the protesting 'farmers'!

Udai Prakash Singh
Art Director posted

Gandhi Chowk Set –
From Ground Zero upwards!

Set is finally ready after three months of back breaking work!

This is what we started with...

The 20 lakh square ft empty field was rented from the government for six months.

It is now... this!

Udai Prakash Singh
Art Director posted

Ajay Devgn

Bang in the middle of the Bhopal, against the masjid, Prakash's art team has built this unbelievably authentic looking city hub.

Kareena Kapoor Khan *says*

I refuse to believe that it isn't a real location! Is everyone just playing a prank on me?!

Arjun Rampal

I went totally trigger happy when I saw the set! Couldn't stop taking pictures!

Prakash Jha *says*

It is a set! We have built even the roads...

Udai Prakash Singh's Blog

ALL SET!

Prakashji called me and said let's see the location. And then we both went and stood in the middle of a vast land. And he casually tells me, yahaan sheher ka chowk banana hai. My jaw dropped. It was an empty field!

I made drawing after drawing, presented scores of elevations to Prakashji. I did not want to leave anything to chance. Once the designs were approved, we set off for Bhopal.

First we laid down roads and lanes. And then filled in the lanes with shops, offices, residential buildings, a temple... and even a movie theatre!

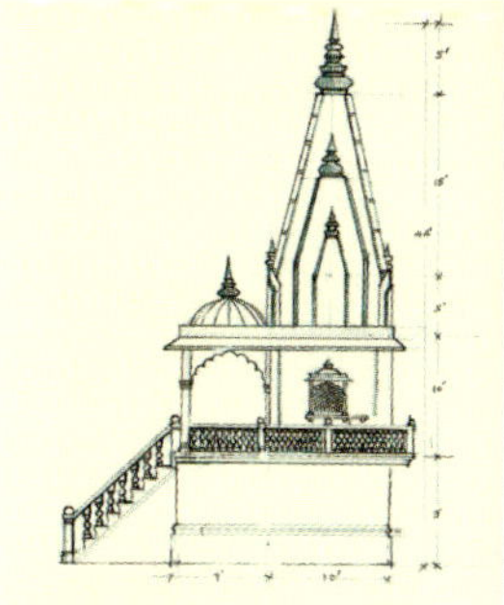

We had plans mounted at the mouth of every 'lane' indicating what was to be built there. One lane was to be built with residential buildings. Another was to look like a bustling city centre. Another was to look like a quiet locality. We used the beautiful Taj-ul-Masjid as the backdrop and around one side of it, brick by brick, we built a town!

This is a gate we built. And then painted it for it to look aged. People who came later on the sets have lost money on bets believing that this gate was real!

These are real local shopkeepers!

They jumped at the opportunity to set up 'branches' of their shops and sell their goods to the entire crew and cast and be on camera! The idea was to make it look as real as possible. So we had everything from a grocery store to a photocopy centre. From an antique goods store to a chaat ka thela!

This is one of the most precious things I created.

Bapu's statue. First made in clay and then in fibre!

It was the first time that I was leading a huge art direction team of almost 175 people. I have surprised even myself. When I look at the city of Ambikapur, sometimes even I refuse to believe that it's a set!

▲ *Dwarka Anand's House*

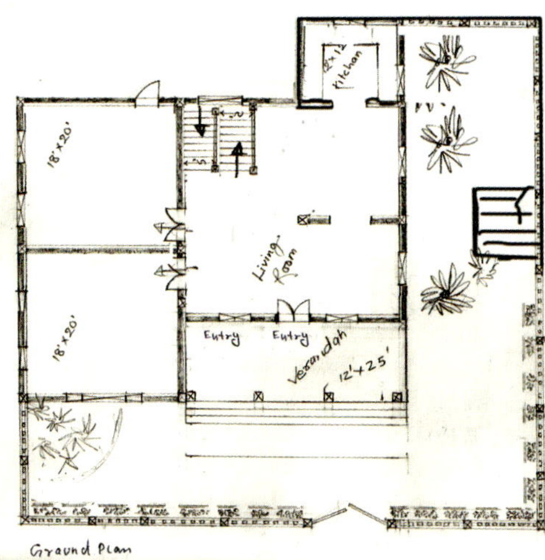

Dwarka Anand's House – Built separately while Gandhi Chowk was being made.

Dhaba At the Highway – Built entirely from scratch in two days flat!

Transformer at Gandhi Chowk – Made with plywood!

Sumitra's Balcony

Lane at Gandhi Chowk

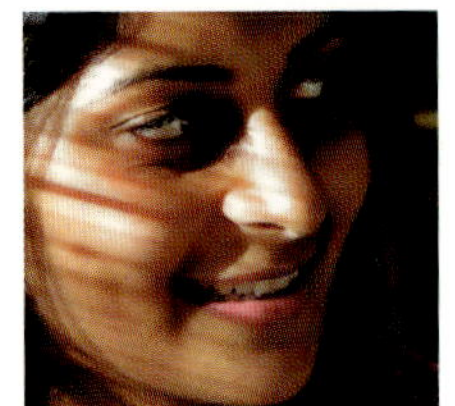

Priyanka Mundada Costume Designer shared an album **KHAADI-ITYAADI**

Prakashji insisted on coming along to pick the khaadi for Mr. Bachchan's costume. So he and I had a nice, girls-day-out kind of shopping afternoon! And as if the shopkeeper wasn't awed enough to see Prakashji, we told him Mr. Bachchan would wear all this khaadi! He was so star struck and happy, we had to physically force the money on him!

Priyanka Mundada
Costume Designer posted

Crisis! Arjun Rampal makes even a simple, locally bought kurta look haute couture! How to dress him down?!

Arjun Rampal likes this.

Priyanka Mundada
Costume Designer posted

Ajay's costumes changed according to the graph of his character. We started with suave suits and tshirts. And when he became more politically inclined, he started wearing bundies and khaadis.

Kareena's style is comfortable yet chic, in this film. She wears shirts and denims mostly but is not a 'jhalli'. So she wears well fitted shirts in crepes and a variety of hues with a nice scarf for some drama.

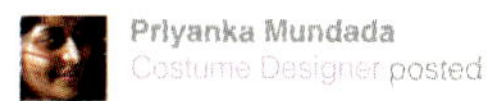

Priyanka Mundada
Costume Designer posted

Kareena and I were both hoping we'd get to experiment with her costumes in the romantic song. But Prakashji has insisted he doesn't want anything to take away attention from the story. So we have to stick to her shirt and denims journo look!

Kareena Kapoor Khan I can't remember the last time my director did NOT want me to look glamourous! LOL!

Priyanka Mundada
Costume Designer posted

Manoj's character was flamboyant. So we gave him flashy watches, materials with a bit of sheen... bright coloured silk kurtas.

Amrita was dressed like a simple homemaker living in a small town. No frills.

The idea was to keep them looking like people we see every day, on the street, in the bus. Not like actors.

GROUP CHAT OF Satyagraha Associate Directors

Ritam *says*

Prakashji has gone mad. He suddenly wants 7000 people on location tomorrow!

Karan Talwar *says*

Arrey we have an army of junior artistes. Should I mobilise them?

Iti Agarwal *says*

But he wants people within the age bracket of 18-30 only! And he wants them to be an angry crowd reacting with frenzy!!! How can we prep 7000 people in a day?!

Karan Talwar *says*

They are already prepared! We did a 3 month workshop with the crowd actors remember? They have been prepped to be angry, sad, happy, screaming, silent...
you name the emotion! They are veterans now!

Ritam *says*

But will you able to communicate to all of them in time?!

Karan Talwar *says*

They are divided into groups. I'll just inform the group heads! They'll do the rest.

NEXT DAY

Karan Talwar
Associate Director

The stellar crowd actors looking suitably angry! Giving stiff competition even to the Angry Young Man!

Prakash Jha

Today is Picnic Day!

Karan Talwar Associate Director
STRICT instructions to all ADs today: No matter how behind schedule we get, NO ONE will shout at the kids!

Iti Agarwal Associate Director
I don't think Prakashji has ever been so particular about how we deal with even the stars on set! These kids are being taken better care of than Mr. Bachchan!

Kareena Kapoor Khan

It was fascinating to watch Prakashji with the kids! He is usually so strict about not wasting time. But with the kids it was almost as if he had forgotten why they were there... He was singing with them, telling them jokes! And we were all like, uh *hello... we have a film to shoot, remember?!*

Sachin Krishn
Cinematographer

But we had the camera rolling all the time and we got most of the shots we wanted with the kids, in between all the fun!

Arjun Rampal
@ArjunRampal
It's a really hot day and we're shooting the water cannons scene! Thank God!
फायर - ब्रिगेड
फोन-101. (2551511)

Arjun Rampal What the....???!!! These water cannons HURT!!!
Kareena Kapoor Khan And how! I feel bruised all over!
Ajay Devgn It didn't help that the water was stinking and dirty! And to make matters worse Prakash very smartly climbed on top of the tank and took the hose in his hands!
Amrita Rao And I used to sometimes watch it being used on people in the news and I would think - do they really expect to scare people away with water?! But now I know better!
Arjun Rampal Yeah! And he kept aiming at our mouths! How exactly are we supposed to say HIS lines?!
SrBachchan But it's something to think about, isn't it? That people who truly fight and protest, stand bravely in the face of such horrible pain and difficulty. If they can do it, why can't we?
Prakash Jha likes this.

Sachin Krishn

Satyagraha is such a topical film on such a relevant subject that I decided to shoot it like a documentary. I restrained the cinematography to keep it in the background and tried not to do anything that would take away the attention from what was being said.

I decided to use hard, direct light on the faces of the actors so the viewer could see what was going on behind their eyes. If you look closely, you might even be able to see the pores on their faces. It's that kind of film. It is saying something that is much larger, much more important than all of us put together.

Sachin Krishn

There was a sense of visual symbolism that we played with. This shot was deliberately composed thus to remind one of Gandhi and create a similar sense of reverence for Dadu's character.

Sachin Krishn

We consciously decided to shoot the climax in cross lighting towards the second half of the day even if it meant shooting over a few more days. The afternoon sun gave the sequence a more gritty texture and mood. It also added to the sense of dipping hope and desperation. Dadu's death scene was shot against the setting sun to create a sense of loss.

Santosh Mandal Editor shared a video

Finally locked the edit of the scene where Manav comes back. Have been at it for days...

This was one of the most difficult sequences to cut. There is a tense build up in which Manav walks through the market, with the crowd that is a hair's breath away from attacking him. And then a taut scene where he confesses to his sins and waits as Dwarka Anand takes his time before he matter-of-factly declares Manav worthy of their trust. And then a brief moment of tenderness. The whole sequence is emotionally tense and sensitive in which Arjun's feelings of betrayal have to be shown, Sumitra's torn faith has to be mirrored and finally Yasmin's bruised love has to bear down on everyone's forgiveness. There was too much to be said. And it was too easy to let it meander. We did several versions of the sequence before we finally locked a cut we were all happy with.

Santosh Mandal Editor shared a video

As always I was on shoot ensuring Bhaiji (as Prakash Jha is addressed by many who work with him) took enough counter shots and cutaways. Ajay would often get irritated with me and say I was taking more shots than required and I wouldn't use any of them.

When the edit got locked the first thing I did was show it to him so he could see I had used almost every single angle we had shot!

Meet Bros Anjjan
uploaded an album **JANTA ROCKS**

We read the lyrics in Prakashji's office and looked at each other. It did not have a conventional pattern. It breaks into a chorus suddenly, at times it becomes a monologue and then out of nowhere it takes on the feel of naarebaazi... It wasn't a song, it was a short story!

Prasoon Joshi

Prakashji told me he wanted something that immediately becomes a mantra for the youth. With this song, I found my writing flowing into various kinds of expression. Perhaps because what we are saying also has so many sides, our subject has so many facets. So the song became a bit of a meandering river....

Prakash Jha I wanted this song to be a reflection of the mad diversity that our 'janta' really is. Of what they are feeling. They believe in themselves. And are ready to bring about a change. And they are faced with so many obstacles, some created even by their own diversity! So I was actually happy about the meandering patterns that seemed to be developing in Prasoon's writing for this song. And I was convinced we were going in the right direction when Meet Bros Anjjan impulsively started jamming right there in my office! The folksy-movement kind of rhythm they brought into the song was just the energy it needed...

Kareena Kapoor Khan It was great fun shooting for this song. With that huge crowd. I felt like I was in a rock concert!

Arjun Rampal This song is trademark Prakash Jha. It talks about the politics of today and is still fun.

Ajay Devgn 'Janta rocks' is such a simple and yet catchy phrase. The youth will feel as if they themselves came up with it!

Indian Ocean

Shooting our song *Hum Bhole The...* in Satyagraha.

When Prakashji came to us the one question we asked him was - why us? And he said because I want a song that connects with the youth.

Prakash Jha There is something about the sound of Indian Ocean which is very 'today' and it is indigenous. Their music somehow speaks to the youth in a language they understand. And what better way to communicate with young India than through the music they understand and love?

Prasoon Joshi

It came from a poem that I had written as a reaction to the India Against Corruption movement, to the fervour that was rising in the country. And when Prakashji and Satyagraha happened, it grew into this song that shows how angry every young Indian is feeling today.

Indian Ocean We usually develop every song over years by singing it differently from time to time in uncut versions to live audiences. And we will do so with this one too. But what we love about it is the energy of this song. It's the kind of song that lights a spark!

Indian Ocean

And, it is our debut on the silver screen!

Aadesh Shrivastava

shared his album RASKE BHARE TORE NAINA

Prakashji was very clear he wanted the flavour of Mora Piya... So I decided to do another classical piece with a lounge rendition. I took the raag darbaari composition and juxtaposed it with modern piano arrangements. We played the electric guitar in a classical way and restrained the tabla and other 'strong' sounds to create a romantic mood...

Ajay Devgn

The way it has been composed and shot, it is electrifyingly sensual. And yet it is so contained and calm. It very nicely portrays the very real and mature love between Manav and Yasmin.

Prakash Jha Aadesh's music always stands out as radically different from everything else. His song Raske Bhare Tore Naina is like an oasis in the film. It comes at a time when emotions are hurting and a sense of anxiety looms large over all the characters. And the song does the work of a warm, soothing, balmy night breeze.

Prasoon Joshi

Setting classical music to a 'lounge sound' is the only way we can share at least some of our rich heritage of classical music with today's youth. I really enjoyed writing this song. You get such few chances to write a 'classical' song these days. Who talks like that, who romances like that any more?

It was shot at the stunning Taj Mahal ruins of Bhopal. But the crew had a terrifying two nights of setting up lights and sets because it is believed that the ruins are haunted! The technicians worked in groups, always staying within sight of each other!

Salim-Sulaiman

shared their album *RAGHUPATI RAGHAV*

We wanted to do a spin on the original version of Raghupati Raaghav Raja Ram and not just set it to modern instrumentation. So based on the chorus melody, we took off into a new song.

Prakash Jha

The meaning of Satyagraha has changed today. It is no longer enough to be able to bear pain. One has to do something to stop it from being inflicted. And we decided to use an already existing song that symbolises Satyagraha and laced it with our theme.

Prasoon Joshi
"Ab tak dheeraj maanga tha, prabhu ab dheeraj matt dena." The frustration, the anger and the desperate prayer for strength to fight it out - that is what the people are praying for today. They are in the middle of a war to protect righteousness. Every day in the common man's life is a war against corruption. Corruption around him, in him.

Amrita Rao *It is such a serious moment in the film. But we had such a blast shooting this song. It was like a night out with music and friends. And we were happily posing away in our cool Nehru topis!*

Ajay Devgn It is such an inspiring song. It makes you think like you never have before. Ever since the song was ready, it plays on loop in my car!

Kareena Kapoor Khan I was amazed at how Prakashji and his team work. Probably for the first time in my career, I have seen an entire song being shot in just six hours!

Salim-Sulaiman We were aware that this is the single most explosive moment in the film when an entire crowd is collectively feeling helpless and angry. And so, we made the music big. There is a sharp decisive tone which we deliberately maintained through the entire piece.

Sachin Krishn

It was a massive lighting set up. We had to light up not only the entire field but also the buildings at the edge of it and show the people sitting on top of it. If we had lit up and shot it in bits, the song would have taken twenty days to finish. So we just lit up the entire place in one go and went in to shoot. The song is a high point in the film. And while we had to stick to the realism, there was a magical sense of hope in the middle of desperation that we needed to create. We lit up the entire ground with a lot of soft glimmering, mood lights. There were sudden bursts of light through the field, almost like bursts of hope.

Prakash Jha

We shot it smoothly in two evenings. We do train the crowds thoroughly. So I know they will perform and create the mood I want. But on those two evenings it was almost as if they understood the relevance of what they were doing. And not just in the film, but in life. The sombre mood of such a gigantic crowd, unified in thought... it was humbling. When I looked at them, my reason for making this film came back to me. People are coming together to start a movement. People ARE coming together to be the change they wish to see.

SATYAGRAHA IS NOT A THING OF THE PAST.

LOST & FOUND
LOST &

Satyagraha The Film

Timeline | **About** | Photos | Friends | More

About Satyagraha The Film

Satyagraha is the story of a bereaved father who finds a son. It is the story of an orphan who finds a father and meaning in life. It is the story of a righteous journalist who suddenly finds love in the middle of a political storm. It is the story of an aspiring politician who suddenly finds a cause to fight for. It is the story of a young woman who dedicates herself to her dead husband's dream. And finally, Satyagraha is the story of how all of them come together in a moment of crisis that erupts from a personal tragedy. And how suddenly, without any of them meaning for it to, this crisis escalates into a massive peoples' movement that they find themselves at the helm of. But are they equipped to handle its consequences? Will they be able to rise to the challenge? Will they be able to lead the people and this movement that has the power to change the course of history...?

Basic Information

Started	August 1, 2011
Release Date	August 30, 2013
Directed by	Prakash Jha
Written By	Prakash Jha, Anjum Rajabali
Starring	Amitabh Bachchan, Ajay Devgn, Kareena Kapoor Khan, Arjun Rampal, Manoj Bajpayee, Amrita Rao
Produced By	Prakash Jha, Ronnie Screwvala, Siddharth Roy Kapur

Prakash Jha

Anjum Rajabali

Amitabh Bachchan

Ajay Devgn

Kareena Kapoor Khan

Arjun Rampal

Manoj Bajpayee

Amrita Rao

Ronnie Screwvala

Siddharth Roy Kapur

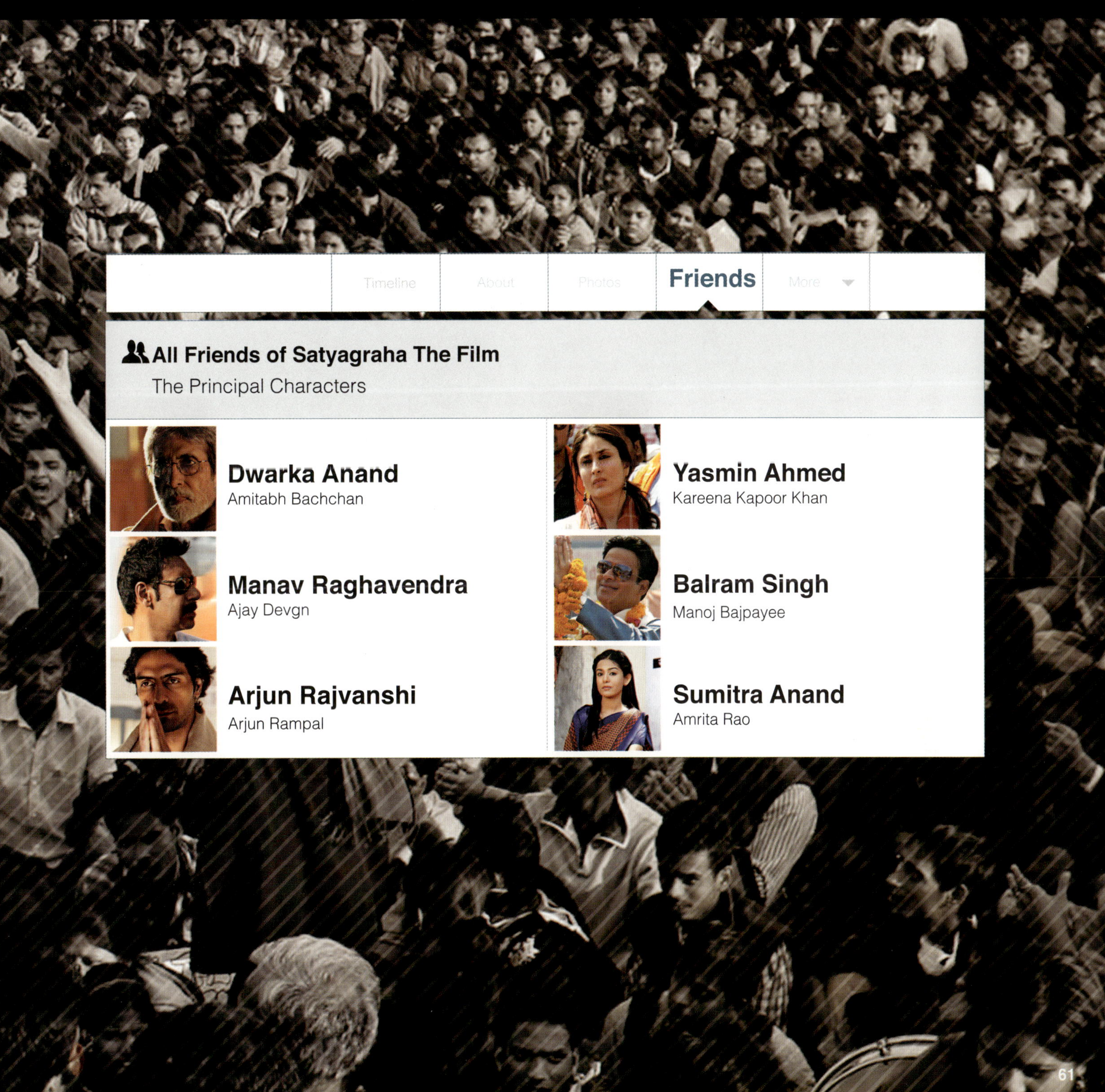
Timeline
About
Photos
Friends
More
All Friends of Satyagraha The Film
The Principal Characters
Dwarka Anand
Amitabh Bachchan
Yasmin Ahmed
Kareena Kapoor Khan
Manav Raghavendra
Ajay Devgn
Balram Singh
Manoj Bajpayee
Arjun Rajvanshi
Arjun Rampal
Sumitra Anand
Amrita Rao

Dwarka Anand

Timeline | About | **Photos** | Friends | More

About Dwarka Anand

Work Retired Teacher

Lives in Ambikapur, India

Lives a quiet peaceful life with his son and daughter-in-law. Runs a small school in his backyard. Is incredibly idealistic, and kind to a fault.

Favourite Quote

"Be the change you wish to see in this world."

– Mahatma Gandhi

Photos of Dwarka Anand

Dwarka Anand

Electricity bills suddenly double! Corruption is seeping into the very roots of our society. Appalled!

Anjum Rajabali Dwarka comes from a tradition that is fast becoming obsolete. He believes in idealism and upholds Gandhi's socialist views. And in that sense is almost a misfit in today's world!

Prakash Jha He is extremely happy that his son has decided to follow his footsteps and taken up a job where he can work for the betterment of the society. He is so staunchly supportive of the growth of the entire society that he almost condemns individual growth.

SrBachchan When Prakash narrated the story to me, I realised that it is going to be a significant comment on what is going on in the world and in our country. Dwarka's unfazed belief in his ideals is inspiring. And playing this character is an honour.

About Manav Raghavendra

Work Telecommunications Conglomerate

Lives in New Delhi, India

Fiercely ambitious and unapologetically successful. He has no reservations in using questionable methods to get what he wants. In just a few years, he has attained the reputation of being a 'rising star of the Indian telecom industry'.

Favourite Quote

"The question isn't who is going to let me. It is who is going to stop me."

– Ayn Rand

Photos of Manav Raghavendra

Manav Raghavendra updated his status

500 million in 5 years!
Now on to the billion!

Anjum Rajabali Manav's character essentially personifies the generation of today that is enmeshed in commerce but is depoliticised. He has worked his way up by bribing officials and ministers, and effectively rendering the government machinery useless.

Prakash Jha And that is the grudge that Dwarka Anand holds against him! That people like him are responsible for bringing the situation to this point. And that this greed for success is the reason for corruption. It is driving the country and society towards ruin. Manav finds Dwarka's ideas old fashioned and amusing. He frankly says greed is good!

Ajay Devgn It's interesting how Manav's character brings out another side of greed and ambition. One that commands respect. It's a sentiment which everyone relates to today. If I work hard for it, I deserve to get more than someone who doesn't.

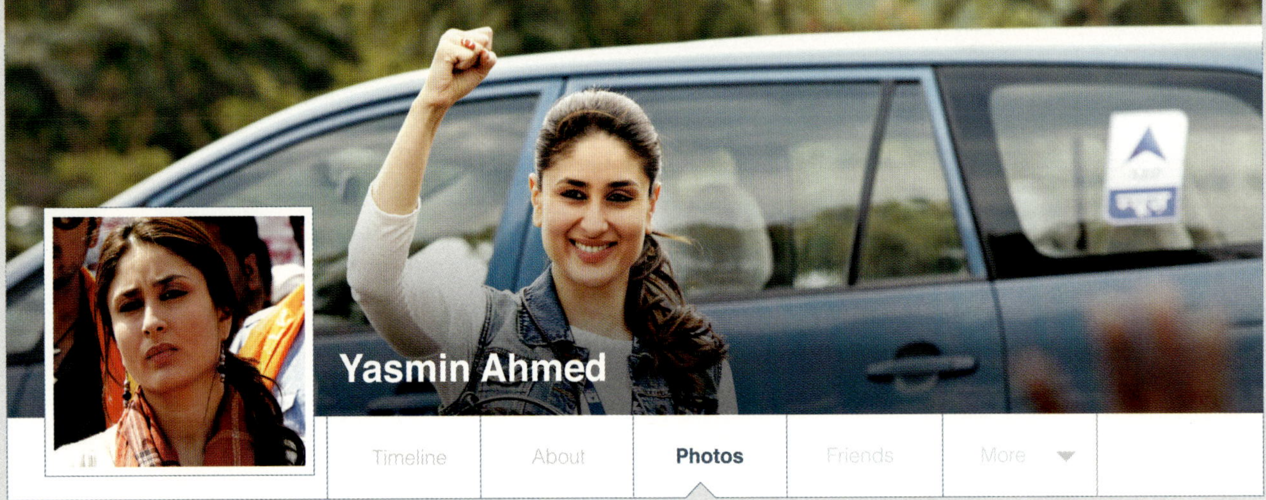

Timeline | About | **Photos** | Friends | More

About Yasmin Ahmed

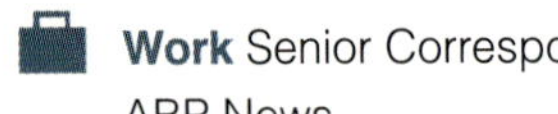

Work Senior Correspondent, ABP News

Lives in New Delhi, India

Completely fearless, she follows the truth, no matter where it leads her. One of the few last people standing in honest journalism.

Favourite Quote

"I became a journalist because I did not want to rely on newspapers for information."

– Christopher Hitchens

Photos of Yasmin Ahmed

Yasmin Ahmed shared a photo

Is the government a landgrabbing mafia in white caps and Nehru jackets?

Prakash Jha Yasmin is the audience's point of view. She asks the questions, refuses to take sides... and simply tries to understand.

Anjum Rajabali Yasmin's character was conceived as the counterpoint. A counterpoint to Manav's individualism, to Arjun's fanaticism and to Dwarka Anand's idealism. Wading through the gutter press around her, she refuses to fall into the muck and reports with unwavering ethical standards. She is the voice of reason.

Kareena Kapoor Khan Through Yasmin's character, I think I have gotten a better understanding of the world around us. Of the times we live in. It was an inspiring character to play.

About Arjun Rajvanshi

 **Work** Youth Leader

 **Lives in** Ambikapur, India

College Dropout. Whatever he does, he does with all his heart. At times without even understanding why. A passion man. Dreams of leading the country one day. Even though he has not a single clue, how to!

Favourite Quote

"No real change in history has ever been achieved by discussions."

– Netaji Subhash Chandra Bose

Photos of Arjun Rajvanshi

Arjun Rajvanshi updated his status

Need at least five thousand people tomorrow at Gandhi Chowk. Cannot let them get away with the bridge collapse so easily. Be there!

Anjum Rajabali Arjun is the local rabble-rouser personifying adventurist violence. He is naive, acts before he thinks and fancies himself as some sort of a Che Guevara! He aims to become a political leader but in truth has no ideological direction. And Manav harnesses his energy, giving it strategic direction.

Prakash Jha At first Arjun does not come across as someone who would be involved in this kind of a movement so passionately. But it becomes clear that he is extremely possessive about his 'area'. He is nursing it, working hard for it and will not tolerate anyone harming it.

Arjun Rampal I found the passion of the man very compelling. If he sets his mind to it, he just goes for it. His political ambition is driven by a genuine desire to lead, not to become a corrupt money making politician. In the current scenario, it is this passion for politics that is the need of the hour.

Timeline | About | **Photos** | Friends | More

 About Balram Singh

Work State Home Minister

 **Lives in** New Delhi/Ambikapur, India

A shrewd businessman rising rapidly in the industry of Indian politics.

Favourite Quote

"I am extraordinarily patient, provided I get my own way in the end."

Margaret Thatcher

"Politics is not a game, it is an earnest business."

– Winston Churchill

"If voting changed anything, they would make it illegal"

– Emma Goldman

Photos of Balram Singh

Balram Singh wrote in his timeline

New Delhi

The idiots really believe they are going to get a lakh each as compensation! LOL! Indians believe anything you say on TV!!!

Anjum Rajabali Balram is unapologetically and unabashedly corrupt. As are almost all politicians in the cowbelt.

Prakash Jha In today's times, politics makes good business sense. Balram has won the election with a lot of effort and investment so that he can earn during his tenure. And has no qualms about this attitude.

Manoj Bajpayee There is a flamboyance about Balram Singh which I enjoyed portraying. He has a twisted sense of humour that comes up unexpectedly in some scenes. He is not only the negative element but also the comic element in the film!

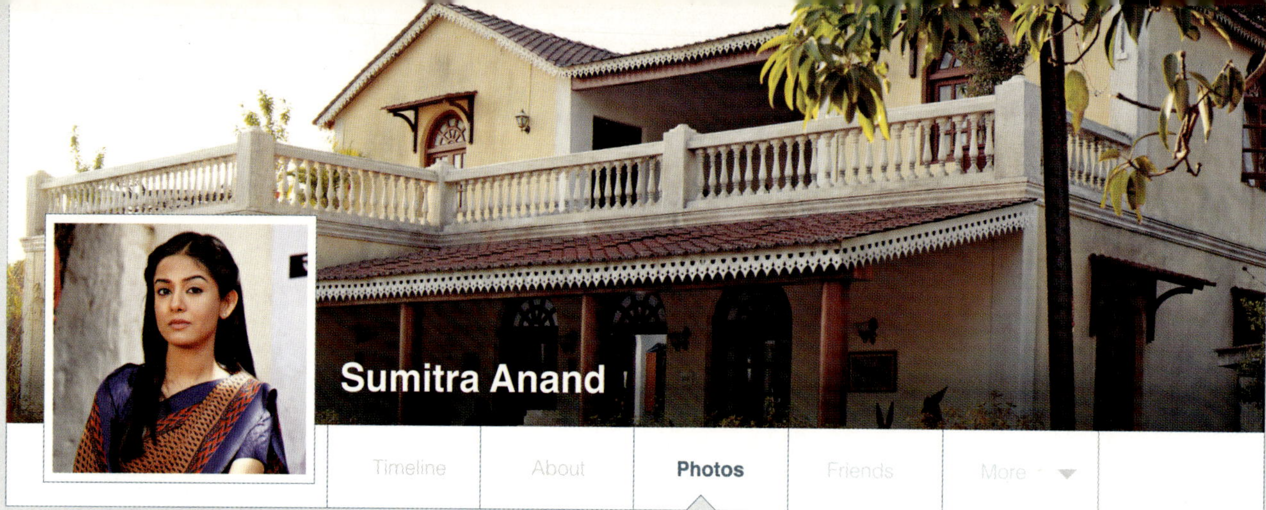

About Sumitra Anand

 **Work** Homemaker

 **Lives in** Ambikapur, India

Lives with a loving husband and a doting father-in-law. Her family is her world. Finds happiness in small things.

Favourite Quote

"A happy family is but an earlier heaven."

– George Bernard Shaw.

"I know of only one duty, and that is to love."

- Albert Camus

Photos of Sumitra Anand

Sumitra Anand updated her status

Making gobhi parathas for breakfast. The husband is going to be a happy man this morning!

Amrita Rao Sumitra might be a homemaker by choice, but she posseses a calm quiet strength. She could have so easily walked away from it all to mourn her loss. But she chooses to fight by her father-in-law's side.

Prakash Jha She becomes the connection between Dwaraka Anand and Manav when they seem to be drifting in opposite directions.

Anjum Rajabali Sumitra is a kind soul, all about compassion. If people are in distress, they should be helped. Period.

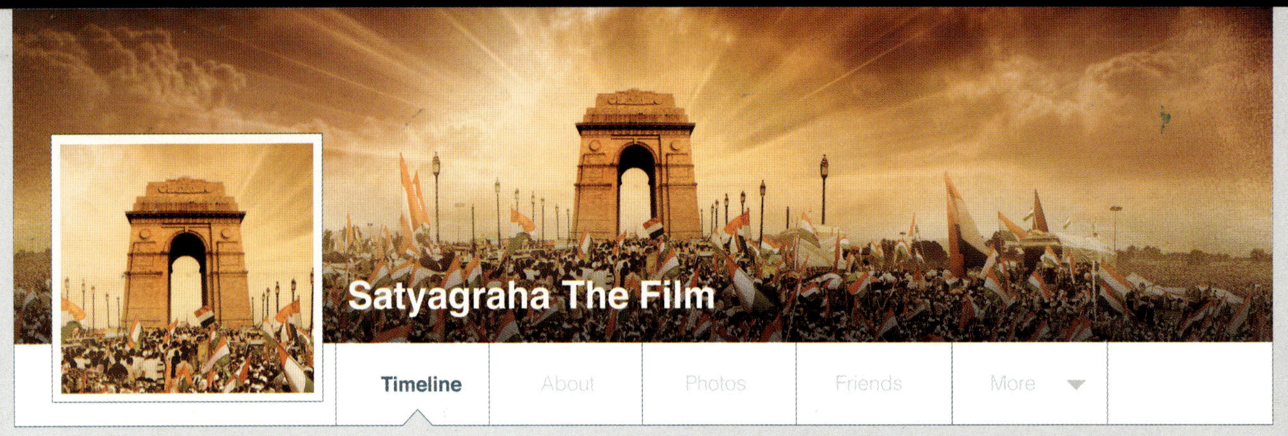

Dwarka Anand

Every day Sumitra comes back empty handed, disheartened. I look at her sad face and feel so helpless. I cannot do anything for my own child?

Satyagraha The Film

Dwarka Anand gives the collector a hard slap across the face. He is now in jail.

Prakash Jha

This is our reality. This is the world we live in where even a Gandhian idealist like Dwarka Anand is driven by his helpless frustration to do something so uncharacteristic! How painful the aftermath must be for him, how painful to live with the fact that he took the law into his hands. This is not his path.

Anjum Rajabali

And yet it is a sentiment that every single person in this country has felt at some point or another. That one blinding moment when your helplessness turns into white hot anger. When reason returns, Dwarka is more than willing to suffer the consequences of his action. But he refuses to apologise!

Prakash Jha

At that time, no one, not even Dwarka has an inkling that this one slap is eventually going to spiral into a movement so huge they will all be sucked into it.

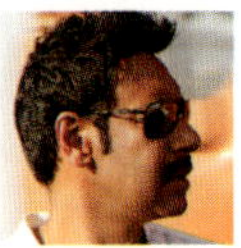

Manav Raghavendra
created **The Ambikapur Revolution Page**

Does this man deserve to be in jail?

Manav Raghavendra answered a poll.

Is Dadu wrong in slapping the collector?

Option	
Yes	▌
No	████████████████
Maybe	█████

Prakash Jha Manav spearheads a movement without intending to, without realising the impact his actions will have. All he wants is to get Dadu out of jail and get the hell out of Ambikapur. Using his corporate experience and expertise, he harnesses every resource from Arjun Rajvanshi to Yasmin Ahmed and creates a sweeping anti corruption frenzy in Ambikapur.

Anjum Rajabali But he is doing it only for sentimental reasons. Because he feels responsible for Dwarka Anand after Akhilesh's death and wants him out of jail at any cost. He doesn't feel an iota of the anti-corruption frenzy that he is spreading amongst the people of Ambikapur!

Dwarka Anand

I refuse to accept the cheque till all the pending dues of Ambikapur are cleared.

Anjum Rajabali Dwarka Anand realises that his compensation is being handed to him simply to quieten the public anger. He takes this opportunity to help all those who have been suffering like him. He could have easily taken the money and walked away. Balram Singh had come hoping to turn this threat into an opportunity. But Dwarka Anand's steadfastness completely turns the table on him.

Prakash Jha His refusal to accept the cheque adds fuel to the fire. And the movement that Manav had started suddenly takes on monstrous proportions, leaving him stumped. And even though he wants to, he is unable to leave.

SrBachchan His refusal brings about a delightful turn of events. After his son's death, Dwarka is shown becoming weak, giving in to anger, feeling helpless. But with Manav's support, the fight comes back in him.

Manav Decides To Stay Back

Prakash Jha The scene where Manav and Dwarka Anand reconcile is my favourite scene. I really enjoyed writing it. The humility, with which the old man apologises and opens his heart to Manav, was very moving.

Anjum Rajabali Manav's untiring efforts make Dwarka realise that his own son would not have been able to do more. His gratitude echoes his regret at having judged Manav too soon. This scene brought about a kind of conversion of Dwarka's rigid ideas. Till now, he had his head stuck in the ideology of the Gandhian days when money and personal growth were not considered virtuous.

Prakash Jha It is also the decisive moment where Manav might not know, but we do, that life will never be the same again. The shrewd businessman has given in to his emotions and has decided to stay back and not go to his billion dollar dream, so that the stubborn old man is not alone.

SrBachchan Every good film has that one scene which when you hear, you tell yourself – I must do this film. The reconciliation scene was that one scene in Satyagraha. There is something so fragile and tender about this moment when two grown men clutch each others' hands and tear up.

Ajay Devgn I agree completely with Amitji. It is beautiful in its simplicity. There are hardly any words said. But the bond of a lifetime is made.

Yasmin Ahmed updated her status

Our meeting with Balram Singh and party was a complete failure. Was shocked at Manav's highhanded and autocratic behaviour.

Balram Singh likes this.

Prakash Jha Despite all his corporate experience and shrewd business sense, Manav has a certain political naivety. And we begin to see glimpses of it now.

Anjum Rajabali The overwhelming support of the crowd has left him inebriated. So his negotiation with the government becomes a personal ego tussle. And Yasmin - the only voice of reason, objects to it. Because she knows that only sound negotiation will translate the crowd's sentiment into any kind of action and change.

Kareena Kapoor Khan It was exciting to be doing something different. The lines I was saying, the sentiments I was supposed to be feeling are all very new to me. I felt I was doing something important!

Ajay Devgn The dichotomy of the character was very interesting to portray. To be involved in something so noble and to be carried away by the power of what you can do... these were fascinating emotions to contemplate...

Satyagraha The Film updated its status

Dadu declares fast unto death!

Prakash Jha When the poor woman challenges Dwarka's decision to not accept the compensation because he is not starving, Dwarka realises that simply dictating terms to the populace will not convince them to not resort to corruption.

Anjum Rajabali And by now Dwarka Anand has acquired enough stature in the public eye, for this declaration to be taken seriously by the government. Dwarka Anand has not declared this fast after political deliberation. And so, this movement is bound to get out of hand at some point.

SrBachchan Satyagraha is such a relevant and topical venture. It throws light on the various issues and events that have affected us in recent times, perhaps lending a better understanding too.

#DaduIs Father of the Nation!
Indian government is crueler than British Raj!
#DaduIs BAPU!
FASTen seatbelts! India is about to change!
We will Fast with Dadu!
#DaduIs a rockstar!
Fourth Day. Respect. #DADUSFAST
Govt take action FAST!
Dadu, this will only weaken you, not them!
System is too SLOW for Dadu's FAST!

STOP POLITICIANS FOOD! Matter will be solved in ONE hour!
Why should only DADU fast? Satyagrahis take turns.
#Satyagraha is the new weapon. Thank you Dadu!
School kids want to fast to fight corruption! #Inspiration #DADUSFAST #SATYAGRAHA
Dadu brings back the weapon of peace. Govt has no choice!
THEY should FAST, not Dadu!
Fasting is Emotional blackmail #DadusFast
The biggest revolution since Freedom Struggle. #DadusFast
Prakash Jha The youth of India today have a unique medium of social communication. And it would be a waste if the social media is unable to bring about a long pending change in the corrupt system.
Anjum Rajabali The people are so fed up and so hungry for change that they are ready to lend their support to the first person who seems capable, even if there is no understanding of how he will make it happen. And we have seen that in the recent times.

Satyagraha The Film updated its status

Dadu weakens with every passing day.

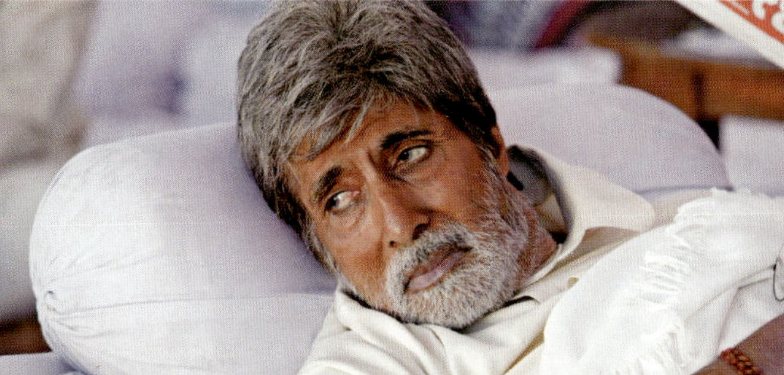

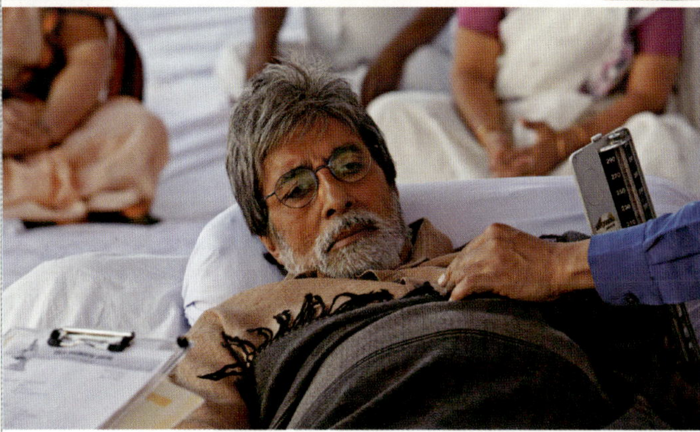

Manav Raghavendra

Feeling very worried. Need a solution really soon.

Prakash Jha With Dwarka Anand's fast Manav is drawn into a waiting game with the government. A game that he is not prepared for. It is a question of who will blink first!

Anjum Rajabali And the government is a past master at it. They know that Manav will not be able to take the pressure of Dadu's deteriorating health. And sure enough, he gives in to one knee jerk reaction after another.

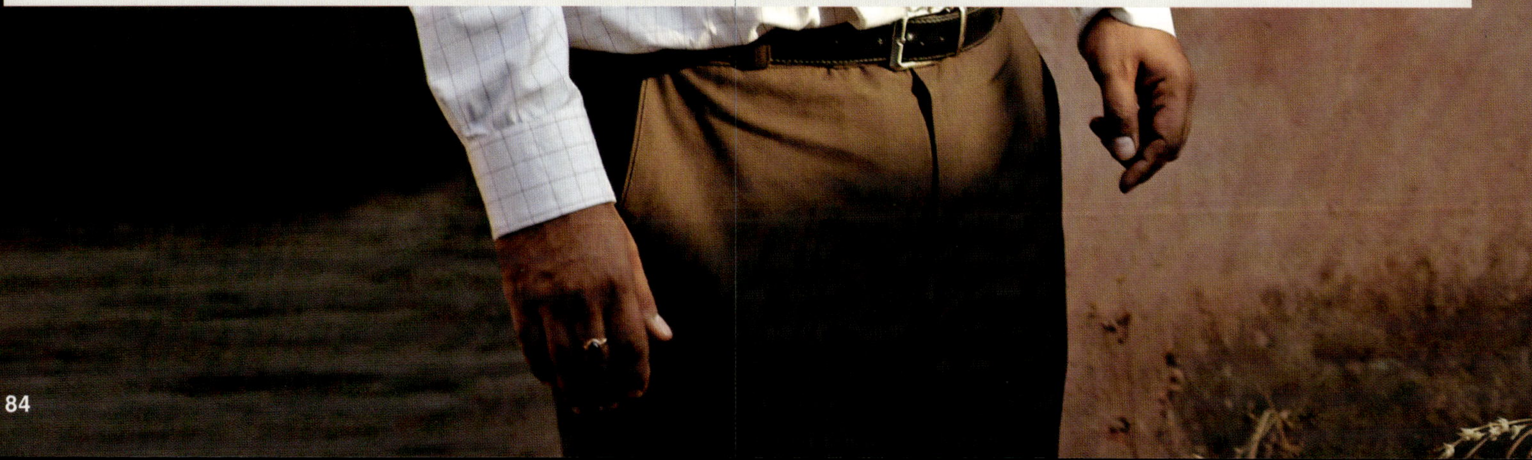

BREAKING NEWS

Manav Raghavendra joins hands with Opposition.

Will this make the government budge?

Balram Singh

LOL! @Manav, you crack me up!

Anjum Rajabali Manav's political naivety comes to open light. He expects to put pressure on the government by joining hands with the opposition party, not realising that if they would have been in power, he would have been fighting with them.

Prakash Jha No political party is genuinely ready to challenge the system. Almost immediately Balram co-opts the Opposition, leaving Manav looking like a prized fool. And he reacts again, deciding to take out Lal Bahadur's shavyatra!

#ManavTheMonster

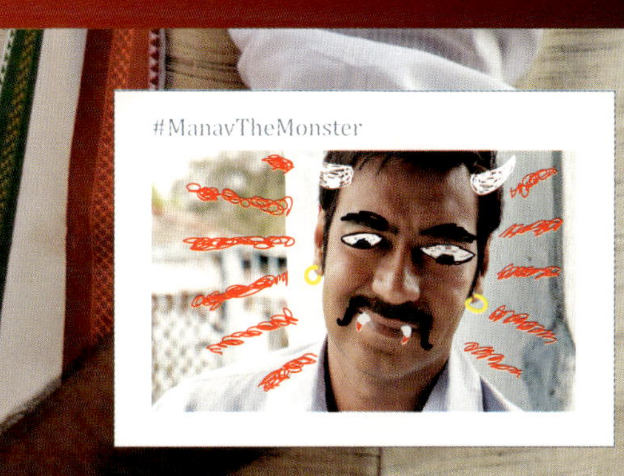

Satyagraha The Film created an album VIOLENCE

AMBIKAPUR BURNS!

The movement goes out of control.

Violence was not our way.

Ruin and disaster await us.

So many sacrifices for more pain and misery

The long battle doesn't seem to end.

Dadu is missing!
Panic spreading amongst the citizens.

The army marches to gun down its own countrymen!

Manav realises what he has done.

DADU
SHOT
DEAD
Satyagraha The Film changed its cover photo

DADU SHOT DEAD

YASMIN AHMED'S BLOG

Ready for Revolution?

There is a black silence that hangs over Ambikapur today. Dadu's death has brought the revolution to a paralysing standstill. But before we think about the way forward, we must first ask ourselves this – were we in truth, ready for this revolution?

It all began with a single slap that was the inevitable expression of helpless frustration at the snail-paced, corruption-infested, incorrigible administration. But thanks to the social media that joins us to one another today, it became breaking news and spread a blazing fire. Today, we have that power. The power to connect. Today the youth of India can come together with just a click.

Can merely converging via posts and likes on Facebook lead to anything of value?

But is this power to unite all that we need? Can merely converging via posts and likes on Facebook lead to anything of value? Where is the ideological and political anchor that is so essential to transform this momentary euphoria of numbers into real and sustainable change? With the country's youth so terribly allergic to politics, are we not uniting in an ideological vacuum? There is no interest, or even curiousity, in how the political system works, in the strengths and limitations of our parliamentary democracy. The solution to this mammoth problem of corruption is actually quite simple: Either we formulate and push through an alternative political system altogether or learn to engage and negotiate with the existing one, to ensure that people-oriented policies and safeguards are instituted using existing democratic systems and protocols?

I'm afraid that until we do this, there will be no real alternative created. And we will remain stuck in this vicious cycle. Our cynicism will only further paralyse us. As a result, we shall look for messiahs. We will blindly trust in them and expect them to wipe out our problems, merely because they proclaim they will. We will of course, lose our capacity to assess their credibility, eager as we are to get seduced by their bombast. It is precisely our distaste for political involvement that will concentrate an inordinate amount of power and moral authority in the hands of those leaders, which will inevitably arouse their latent megalomania and narcissism – no matter how well-intentioned their beginnings were - which will destroy whatever pretenses they had displayed for selfless service! So, when even they fail, as they are bound to, we shall then resort to our favourite pastime of complaining on social media, and at best, resort to those candlelight vigils and marches, which last all of two days. And, like those candles in the wind, our wispy outrage will be extinguised by our own eagerness to go back to our malls, our all-consuming need for personal growth which we usually measure in terms of material lifestyle.

Our cynicism will only further paralyse us. As a result, we shall look for messiahs.

Look at our own case. Manav began this revolution purely for one personal motive: To free Dadu from the prison where he had been unjustly incarcerated. Manav never dreamt that this would snowball into a people's movement based on some larger agenda of bringing accountability into governance. Even Dadu's decisions - to not accept the cheque, and later to go on an indefinite fast – were simply out of the compassion that we all know him for. Neither was a strategist, and more importantly, neither realised that it is only through a deep political involvement – in ideology and in the system – that their objectives can be really fulfilled. A revolution cannot be fuelled merely by good intentions in a political vacuum. Arjun, the most passionate among us all, too was a victim of his own overpowering need for quick solutions, without the understanding of the arduous nature of systemic change.

A revolution cannot be fuelled merely by good intentions in a political vacuum.

These were our leaders. They are the best human beings that I have come across and the best friends that I will ever have. But, and this bears repetition, mere goodness is not enough for leading such a promising movement. Personality cults do not result in revolutions. They end in autocracy.

To labour this point just a tad further: Just look at the methods and tactics we used. We believed that since we had the support of all our locals, all we had to do was demand a change in policies, insist on ordinances. And we actually believed that handing out 'to-do lists' would do the trick!! When the government began using its delaying and diversionary tactics, we raved and ranted. And, issued threats. And, when even that failed, we thought we could blackmail them by fasting-unto-death. When that posed a risk to Dadu's life, we had absolutely no clue how to break the deadlock. And then began the knee-jerk reactions. We made a pact with the devil himself – the Hindu fundamentalist right-wingers – whose very raison d'etre is to rule via the route of hatred and creating hostility for the minorities and backward castes. Manav, who had a terrific talent for negotiations, given his experience within the corporate world, believed that that would be enough to deal with these politicians. But his lack of political understanding and negotiations made that skill boomerang against himself, and all of us.

One might argue that Gandhi used personal fasting as a weapon against the British. Sure. But Gandhi had a superior understanding of politics,and he had conceived of a model for an indigenous political system which he believed was more humane and just. He used fasting as a sharp political weapon to create that system. Not as a tool to offload his moral guilt. Dadu, who will live on in all our hearts as the burning desire for a better tomorrow, was a deeply compassionate man. But, unlike Gandhi, he was no politician. He went on a fast out of kindness and solidarity, but without a plan! He had Gandhi's selfless compassion but lacked his political understanding. It seems futile and rhetorical to repeat this, but India does need a new-age Gandhi. Someone who can reinvent the strategy of non-violent Satyagraha and marry it into the the age of new economics that we live in. I know that I'm sounding like a dreamer, but at the end of this long and tragic struggle, I myself am devoid of further thoughts.

India does need a new-age Gandhi.

But, not of hope. I hope that a political party will emerge from this experience, which will be based on a clearly defined political ideology, and then actually get into the electoral stream and fight to gain legislative and parliamentary power. Without compromising on its principles. I hope that those principles will find expression in clear and uncompromising objectives. I hope that there will be an unambiguously defined action plan to strive for those objectives. I hope that this whole formulation will be driven by sincerity and consistency, using democratic means of decision-making. I hope that we shall remain connected with India's socio-political and economic reality. I hope that we shall never ever seek an alliance with hate-mongers and fundamentalists. I hope that the transparency, accountability that we expect from the government will be practised in our own party. I hope that we will unflinchingly uphold our integrity even if we do not win a single seat. I hope that no matter how difficult it makes the journey, we shall not dilute our agenda into populist declarations. I hope that one day people will be able to trust us. I hope that one day we will be able to lead this country into a better, brighter and just tomorrow.

…people get the leaders that they deserve.

Am I being idealistic? Perhaps. But it really is the only way. Only if people become more aware of their rights and responsibilities as voters, if they stop seeing themselves as mere consumers and reclaim their identity as citizens, will they be actively concerned about not just the actions of their leaders, but also their duty to exercise safeguards and controls to prevent anti-people actions. Only through political awareness will they be able to ensure that leaders are servants of the people, and not masters. A colleague cynically commented that people get the leaders that they deserve. I couldn't agree with this more. Ignorant people get charlatans as leaders. Apathetic people receive callous and selfish politicians. So what does corruption in the ranks of our leadership show about us? Corruption has seeped into our very souls. We expect that the government be uncorrupt, but we want the option to be corrupt, conveniently open to ourselves.

Dadu has left a wisp of hope in our hearts. But if we are not prepared to take the inconvenient, difficult road to a corrupt free India, that wisp of hope will be blown out like a candle in the wind. And then there will be only darkness. And, exploitation. Injustice. And, violence. And every now and then a Dadu will sacrifice himself in vain and all we will do again, is simply ask ourselves – are we ready for a revolution? Are we, in truth, ready for Satyagraha?

SATYAGRAHA

THE STORY BEHIND THE REVOLUTION

THE SCRIPT

PRAKASH JHA
ANJUM RAJABALI

EXT AMBIKAPUR RAILWAY STATION - DAY

A train stops at Ambikapur Railway Station. Manav, gets off the train and is received by Akhilesh.

AKHILESH
Manav!

MANAV
Bloody hell! You're yet to lose your milk teeth and here you are getting engaged! Made me suffer 17 hours in the train!

AKHILESH
You are not used to getting off airplanes and Mercedes... Now try the local auto. Guaranteed free body massage!

EXT AMBIKAPUR STREETS - DAY

An auto wades through the streets of Ambikapur.

MANAV
Tell me, did you meet her?

AKHILESH
Who?

MANAV
The buffalo in Pandey's stable! Your Sumi!

AKHILESH
Oh! So Sumitra's become Sumi, eh?

MANAV
You just wait and watch what else I am going to change!

AKHILESH
Where does she stay? In this lane itself... but we can't meet her right now.

MANAV
Why not? Give me the phone.
(Snatches the phone and dials her number)
Who's stopping you? Your Moghul dictator?

AKHILESH
Right now there are many guests at her place.

AKHILESH
Manav!

MANAV
अबे साले... दूध के दाँत झड़े नहीं अभी और मँगनी करवा रहा है अपनी... 17 घण्टे... Train में रगड़वा दिया...

AKHILESH
तेरी आदत नहीं है न हवाई जहाज और Mercedes से नीचे उतरने की... अब अम्बिकापुर के Autorickshaw में चढ़... पूरे Body की Free Massage हो जायेगी...

MANAV
ये बता उससे मिला कि नहीं?

AKHILESH
किससे?

MANAV
पांडे जी के तबेले की भैंस को!... अरे यार तेरी सुमी से!

AKHILESH
अच्छा... तूने सुमित्रा को सुमी बना दिया!

MANAV
अभी देखता जा उसे क्या–क्या बनाता हूँ... कहाँ रहती है?...

AKHILESH
घर तो उसका इसी सड़क पर है पर... अभी मिल नहीं सकते...

MANAV
क्यूँ? अरे Phone ला...
(Snatches the phone and dials her number)
तेरे मुग़ले आज़म ने मना किया क्या?...

AKHILESH
अरे मेहमान सब भरे हैं उसके यहाँ यार...

MANAV
Please stop the auto... Stop!

MANAV
ए भइया Auto रोक –Auto रोक...

As the phone rings Manav is looking at the houses around. He catches Akki's eyes which have got fixed on the first floor of a building, and tells the Rickshaw to stop.

EXT. SUMITRA'S HOUSE - DAY

Sumitra comes to the balcony looking for Akhilesh. As she appears in the balcony Manav steps out of the rickshaw.

SUMITRA *(On phone)*
Where are you?

SUMITRA *(On phone)*
कहाँ हो तुम ?

AKHILESH *(trying to stop Manav)*
MANAV, No...

AKHILESH *(trying to stop Manav)*
मानव, रुक...

MANAV *(to Akhilesh)*
Wow! She's lovely!

MANAV *(to Akhilesh)*
Wow! She's lovely यार...

SUMITRA
Where are you?

SUMITRA
आप हैं कहाँ?

MANAV *(On Phone)*
Standing right in front of you, and still you can't see me?

MANAV *(On Phone)*
चिराग़ तले अँधेरा... अरे आपके सामने तो खड़ा हूँ...

Sumitra is baffled for a moment. She realises this must be Manav but continues to feign ignorance.

SUMITRA *(to Manav)*
Who are you?

SUMITRA *(to Manav)*
आप हैं कौन?...

Now that they've seen each other Manav switches off the phone and speaks to Sumitra directly.

MANAV
Well... that's the problem with women these days. Online - they recognise you instantly... And when you confront them, they ask 'Who are you?' I am the new police officer of this neighborhood.

MANAV
ये लो... आजकल की लड़कियों का यही Problem है... Online तो सब पहचान लेती हैं... और जब सामने आओ... तो 'कौन हैं आप?'... अरे मैं आपका नया थानेदार हूँ...

SUMITRA
Oh! Mr. police officer. Kindly note my complaint then. The one who is hiding in the auto hasn't come to see me since last evening.

SUMITRA
आ... तो Mr. थानेदार... फ़ौरन हमारा रपट लिखिए... वो जो चुपके से Autorickshaw में बैठे हैं... वो कल शाम हमें मिलने क्यूँ नहीं आये...

MANAV
Forget about him! I am here.

MANAV
अजी उनको छोड़िए – मैं आ गया हूँ ना...

SUMITRA
First get him arrested, then we can also think of meeting.

SUMITRA
पहले इन्हें Lock-up में बंद कीजिए... फिर आपसे भी मिल लेंगे...

A SPECTACLE OF MYSELF!

Costume Designer Priyanka Mundada took about thirty to forty looking glasses for Mr.Bachchan's look test. After politely trying them all on, he requested to use his own!

Akhilesh peeps out at this.

AKHILESH
Come on.

AKHILESH
चल यार...

MANAV *(to Akhilesh)*
She is a smart one.

MANAV *(to Akhilesh)*
मैं न बोलूँ छोरी बहुत Smart है...

Just as Akhilesh begins to pull Manav into the Auto, Transformer Baba appears.

BABA
Reading texts the world walks towards death, but none became wise...
The one, who reads four letters of love, becomes wise.

BABA
पोथी पढ़–पढ़ जग मुआ, पंडित भया न कोय...
ढाई आखर प्रेम का – पढ़ै सो पंडित होय...

MANAV
Who is he?

MANAV
कौन है ये यार?...

AKHILESH
Come, sit.

AKHILESH
अरे चल बैठ यार...

He comes in so suddenly and close to Manav, he is completely taken aback. While Akhilesh pulls out some money and gives to Transformer Baba.

SUMITRA *(explains)*
He is our Transformer baba.

SUMITRA *(explains)*
ये हमारे Transformer Baba हैं...

EXT GANDHI CHOWK DAY

As the rickshaw makes its way through the streets.

AKHILESH (OS)
There is a transformer near the roundabout He has made himself a home there

AKHILESH (OS)
बरसों से इस गाँधी चौक पर जो Transformer है न... उसी के नीचे घर बना लिया है इसने...

MANAV
Ok.

MANAV
अच्छा!

DWARKA HOUSE – EXT COLONY: MORNING

Dwarka is taking to task the Private Electricity Company employees who have come to disconnect the electricity of the local community building and some houses...

DWARKA *(Booming)*
So, now you will teach me about the law?!

DWARKA *(Booming)*
अच्छा... तो अब आप हमें कानून सिखाएँगे?...

LINESMAN
Look...

LINESMAN
देखिये –

DWARKA
No, You look! What is this?
(pointing to the school)
A school! For underprivileged slum kids. What the government should be doing, we are. With funds raised from locals.

DWARKA
पहले आप देखिये... ये क्या है?...
(pointing to the school)
School!...ग़रीब... झुग्गी–झोपड़ी के बच्चों के लिये... जो काम सरकार को करना चाहिए... वो हम सब मुहल्ले वाले चन्दा इकट्ठा कर के चला रहे हैं...

LINESMAN
Whatever! But, you don't pay the bill, we disconnect your line.

LINESMAN
वो जो भी है ठीक है... अगर आप Bill नहीं भरेंगे... तो Line तो काटना पड़ेगा ना...

DWARKA
Is this a bill or blatant loot?
(points to the bill in his hand)
Rs. 600 in June. And this month, Rs. 2700!

DWARKA
ये... ये Bill है – या सरासर लूट?
(points to the bill in his hand)
June में छः सौ रुपया... और... आज... ये देखिए... सत्ताइस सौ रुपया!...

Manav and Akhilesh arrive at Dwarka's colony where there is a huge commotion.

AKHILESH
Looks like someone's got in Dad's way again today!

AKHILESH
लगता है आज फिर बाबूजी के हत्थे चढ़ा कोई...

DWARKA
Ever since electricity got privatized, these companies have made our life hell!

DWARKA
ये जबसे Private Electric Company ने ठेका लिया है... हम सबके नाक में दम कर रक्खा है आपने...

Others standing behind him also begin voicing their protest that they too have been receiving inflated bills.

NEIGHBOUR
Everyone's bills have just doubled, Dadu.

NEIGHBOUR
मुहल्ले में सभी का Bill double से ज़्यादा हो गया दादू जी...

DWARKA
Look at this!

DWARKA
ये देखिए...

On seeing the aggression, the linesman beats a retreat.

LINESMAN *(muttering)*
Suit yourself. Don't pay. I will report it.

LINESMAN *(muttering)*
तो ठीक है – मत भरिए Bill... हम भी लिख देंगे Report...

DWARKA
Report all you want. But, until such billing is rectified, we won't pay!

DWARKA
हाँ–हाँ जो लिखना है आपको लिखिये... लेकिन जब तक आप Meter ठीक नहीं करेंगे... हम भी Payment नहीं करने वाले...

As he turns around flushed, he sees Akki who is standing there with Manav.

AKKI *(introducing Manav)*
Dad... Manav.

AKKI *(introducing Manav)*
बाउजी... मानव...

MANAV
Greetings.

MANAV
नमस्ते!

Dwarka does a 'Namaste'.

DWARKA
Greetings.

DWARKA
Welcome.

DWARKA HOUSE – INT: DAY

Manav, Dwarka and Akhilesh are eating breakfast together.

DWARKA *(asking Manav)*
So, young man. What're your plans for the future.

Manav, who has been enjoying the parathas has his mouth full and gestures with his hands – a flying airplane. Akhilesh answers for him..

AKHILESH
He's going to America, Dad. For his PG.

MANAV
I will setup my own telecom company, when I return.

AKHILESH
Manav has a terrific business-sense, Dad.

DWARKA *(Disgusted)*
Business!! What is wrong with today's young people?! Obsessed with money!

Manav hardly notices the sarcasm.

MANAV
Uncle, money makes the world move! The hunger for profit boosts competition. And competition throws up the best talent. Simple!

DWARKA *(Smiling indulgently)*
Noble-sounding words, indeed! But, the simple truth is that people like you are plain greedy.

Akhilesh starts coughing involuntarily, thoroughly embarrassed at this direct hit. Dwarka notices, but Manav is impervious to the attack.

MANAV
Absolutely! Greed is the engine of growth! That's how the world progresses.

Dwarka does a 'Namaste'.

DWARKA
हाँ, नमस्ते...

DWARKA
आइए... स्वागत है...

DWARKA *(asking Manav)*
So.. Young man... क्या Plans हैं आपके Future के?...

AKHILESH
अ... America जा रहा है बाउजी – P.G. करने...

MANAV
और वापस आकर अपनी Company setup करूँगा... Tele communications...

AKHILESH
मानव का Business sense बहुत अच्छा है बाउजी –

DWARKA *(Disgusted)*
Business!... इह्!... क्या हो गया है आजकल के नौजवानों को... पैसे के पीछे पागल हैं...

MANAV
Uncle, पैसे से ही तो दुनिया आगे बढ़ती है... मुनाफ़े की भूख से Competition बढ़ता है... और Competition से Best Talent निकल कर आता है... Simple

DWARKA *(Smiling indulgently)*
कहने में तो... ये शब्द बड़े महान लगते हैं... लेकिन... सच बात तो ये है कि... आप जैसे लोग... लालची हैं!...

MANAV
बिलकुल!... लालच ही तो Growth का Engine है... उसी से तो दुनिया आगे बढ़ती है!...

For once, Dwarka is at a loss for words..

DWARKA

Enging of growth indeed! Never heard such poppycock!

DWARKA

विकास का Engine!... क्या... क्या बकवास है ये!...

MANAV

Just think. Without greed, why would anyone work hard? Today it's quite simple, uncle: Greed, profit, money, these are not bad words! They lead to development! And the private sector really understands this. Look at them: neat, clean, brimming with energy, And, government offices: Steeped in corruption!

MANAV

सोचिए... लालच नहीं होगा तो आदमी मेहनत क्यों करेगा!... आज का Funda clear है... आगे बढ़ना... लालच, मुनाफ़ा, पैसा... ये सब बुरे शब्द नहीं हैं... इसी से तो विकास होता है... और ये... Private Sector खूब समझता है... आप किसी भी... Private Business में देख लीजिए... Neat clean और Energy से भरा... और सरकारी दफ़्तर!... भ्रष्टाचार से लबालब...

Akhilesh is getting more and more uncomfortable as he sees his father's face getting darker. Manav on the other end is enjoying his breakfast, and the argument.

DWARKA

There's any one cause of corruption: Greed! Strikes like a tsunami. The businessman's greed for illegitimate profits. The broker's greed for shortcuts. The government official's greed for extra income. You may not accept it, but fact is that greedy people like you are destroying not only our country's economy but also our inherent values. Like a cancer!

DWARKA

देखिए... भ्रष्टाचार का केवल एक ही कारण है... लालच!... एक... Tsunami की तरह... Businessman का ग़लत मुनाफ़े का लालच... सौदा करने वाले का Short cut लालच... सरकारी दफ़्तरों में... जो अधिकारी हैं उनकाऽऽ Extra आमदनी का लालच... ये बात आप नहीं मानेंगे... लेकिन सच्चाई ये है... कि आप जैसे लोगों का लालच ही न केवल इस देश की Economy को... बल्कि... हमारी नैतिक विचारधारा को – एक Cancer की तरह नष्ट कर रहा है...

Manav is taken aback at this intense diatribe..

MANAV

Whoa whoa... Chill, Uncle...

MANAV

Whoa whoa... Chill, Uncle...

DWARKA *(Unstoppable now)*

Pardon me, but..

DWARKA *(Unstoppable now)*

माफ़ कीजिएगा भाई साब आप येऽऽऽ...

Akhilesh finally takes action. He intentionally spills a jug full of fruit juice over the table toppling all over Manav's clothes while serving him. Manav immediately gets up reflexively..

AKHILESH

I'm so sorry. Go change, please..

AKHILESH

Sorry, Sorry Sorry यार... तू... तू Change कर लेना –

MANAV

Its Ok.

MANAV

Its Ok.

The distraction has effectively aborted the argument. Dwarka is looking directly at his son, who is of course, avoiding his eyes..

EXT DWARKA HOUSE TERRACE- NIGHT

Later that evening on the terrace, Manav pulls out a hip flask from his back pocket and offers it to Akki.

AKHILESH *(startled)*
Hey, what're you doing? You're crazy. If Dad..

MANAV
Hypocrite! Why are you so scared of your Mughal dictator?

AKHILESH *(smiles)*
It's not that!
(takes a swig)
Without you, I seem to have lost all my bad habits!

Akki puts the flask on the table.

MANAV
I can understand that you don't drink or smoke because of your pop. What I can't is your National Highways obsession. Just look at your qualifications!
(picks up the flask)
And, 35 years later, when you retire, what will you have? 3-4-5 lakhs of savings and pension?
(takes a swig)
Won't even fetch you a decent car then!

Akki laughs as he takes the flask into his hand.

AKHILESH
Who wants a car? After I retire, my dream is to open a small school. And, teach children.

Akki takes another large swig from the hip flask.

MANAV *(takes the flask back)*
Easy, easy..

Akki gives the flask to Manav -

AKHILESH
And before that, I want to make top class roads for the government. Good highways will spur progress. I'm happy, Dad's happy. What else do I want?

MANAV *(laughs and takes a swig)*
This old man will ruin you! You'll waste your life in cubic meters of concrete..

AKHILESH *(startled)*
अबे क्या कर रहा है यार – पागल हो गया है... बाउजी –

MANAV
Hypocrite साला...तू अपने मुग़ले आज़म से इतना डरता क्यूँ है!

AKHILESH *(smiles)*
अरे नहीं यार!...
(takes a swig)
तेरे बिना सारी बुरी आदतें ही छूट गयीं –

MANAV
तू अपने बाप के डर से Cigarette शराब नहीं पीता – I can understand... लेकिन ये जो तेरा... National Highway वाला Funda है ना, ये समझ में नहीं आता... अबे... अपनी Qualifications देख...
(picks up the flask)
सोच... 35 साल बाद जब तू Retire होगा तो क्या मिलेगा... तीस–चालीस–पचास लाख रुपये की Pension और Provident Fund...
(takes a swig)
उसमें तो उस वक़्त एक अच्छी गाड़ी भी नहीं आएगी...

AKHILESH
अबे गाड़ी किसको चाहिए!... अपना तो सपना है Retirement के बाद एक छोटा सा School बनाउँ... और बच्चों को पढ़ाउँ –

MANAV *(takes the flask back)*
ए एऽऽऽ... Neat है यार...

AKHILESH
और उससे पहले First Class रास्ते बनाउँ सरकार के लिये... अच्छे Highways बनेंगे तो उन्नति होगी देश की... मैं खुश... बाबूजी भी खुश... बस यार, और क्या चाहिए! –

MANAV *(laughs and takes a swig)*
बुड्ढा मरवाएगा तेरे को... सारी उमर धूल खायेगा – और ज़िन्दगी भर Cubic Meter Concrete गिनता रहेगा...

MANAV *(puts the flask abck on the table)*
You'll never change! See, my target is clear: 500 million in 5 years, a billion in 10.
(Akhilesh takes a swig from the flask.)
India is the fastest growing market and I want to maximize every opportunity.

MANAV *(puts the flask abck on the table)*
तू कुत्ते की दुम है!... देख, अपना Funda Clear है... 500 million in 5 years - One Billion in Ten...

India is the fastest growing market and I want to maximise every opportunity...

MANAV *[contd.]*
It's still not too late. Put this engagement, wedding, Sumitra business on the back burner, and come with me.

MANAV *[contd.]*
अभी भी Chance है... ये मँगनी–शादी–सुमित्रा... सबको डाल Waiting List पर... और चल मेरे साथ...

Akhilesh laughs at Manav's teasing. But suddenly Akki notices Dwarka standing there and stops laughing. They both look stunned and stand up as Dwarka steps forward. Akhilesh quickly hides the flask into the roots of the plants.

Dwarka continues to coldly look at both of them.. Manav finally steps forward, putting his arm around Akhilesh.

MANAV
Let me take you to your room..

MANAV
चल तुझे कमरे तक छोड़ दूँ...

Dwarka's quiet voice booms..

DWARKA
Thank you. But, Akhilesh is not so drunk on your spurious dreams, that he can't even walk to his room. I will be obliged if you will now just let him be.

DWARKA
धन्यवाद आपका... अब इतना भी मुनाफ़े के नशे में नहीं डूबा अखिलेश... कि वो अपने कमरे तक खुद चल भी ना सके... अब आप इन्हें यहीं छोड़ दें तो... मेहरबानी होगी...

He looks hurt and baffled. Akhilesh comes to his rescue.

AKHILESH
Dad, Manav did not mean...

AKHILESH
बाबूजी... मानव ने ऐसा कुछ भी...

Dwarka cuts him in sharply –

DWARKA
I can see.. what he's done to you in such a short time. These are their tricks, son. To trap you in a billion dollar mirage. And, the only way out of these illusory heights is down. Crash land!

DWARKA
हाँ, वो तो मैं देख ही रहा हूँ कि... इतनी ही देर में इन्होंने... क्या बना दिया है आपको... ये सब इनकी चाल है बेटा... इनके Billion Dollar.. माया जाल में तुम्हें फँसाने की... और जिन सफलता की उँचाइयों के सपने ये दिखाएँगे तुम्हें, वहाँ से निकलने का बस एक ही रास्ता है नीचे... नीचे जाने का...

Manav is stunned... and pained.

MANAV
I don't know why you're so bitter about the idea of success.

MANAV
पता नहीं... आपके अन्दर इतनी कड़ुआहट क्यों है... Success को लेके...

DWARKA
You will obviously never understand that because money is your only religion. And, the market your morality. Country, society,

DWARKA
ये बात शायद आप लोगों की समझ में कभी नहीं आयेगी... क्योंकि पैसा ही आपका धर्म है... और बाज़ार आपकी Morality!... देश... समाज... मानवता

service of humanity – these don't figure in your dictionary. All you know how to do is grab! The ultimate consumers. For your class, scams and frauds are par for the course. You're eating into the very core of this country.

की सेवा के मूल्य ये सब... आपकी Dictionary में हैं ही नहीं... दुनिया से आप लोग सिर्फ़... लेना जानते हैं... The Ultimate Consumer... ये Scams... घोटाले... इससे कोई फ़र्क नहीं पड़ता आप जैसे Class के लोगों को... खोखला करते जा रहे हैं आप लोग इस देश को...

Manav looks devastated.

Manav looks devastated.

DWARKA
But I'm happy that in spite of you, Akhilesh hadn't lost his values.

DWARKA
लेकिन मुझे इस बात की खुशी है कि... आपकी संगत में रहने के बावजूद... मेरे अखिलेश के मूल्य नहीं बदले...

It is almost as if Dwarka has dismissed Manav.. With his heart heavy as lead, Manav turns to leave. Akhilesh hestiates but only for a moment, and follows Manav.

EXT DWARKAS HOUSE NIGHT

Moments later Manav has come out with his bag packed. Both have tears in their eyes as they come to a Rickshaw.

AKHILESH
Please forgive him, Mannu.. He doesn't understand you..

AKHILESH
माफ़ कर देना बाबूजी को मन्नू – वो समझते नहीं तुमको...

MANAV
It's okay pal. I don't understand him either.

MANAV
Its Ok यार... मैं भी कहाँ समझता हूँ उनको...

As Manav begins to get into the Rickshaw he turns to Akhilesh...

MANAV
And listen, please explain to Sumi.
(to Rickshaw guy)
Let's go.

MANAV
और सुन... सुमि को समझा देना...
(to Rickshaw guy)
चलो भइया...

Akhilesh understands as he nods. He stands there watching as Manav's rickshaw drives away.

TITLE SEQUENCE:

EXT NIGHT CLUB NIGHT

3 YEARS LATER...

As Manav enters the nightclub, the atmosphere is electric. An exquisite dancer is putting up a show while Manav mingles with his business associates.

Just as they are grooving to the intoxicating music a seductively dressed woman, Malini Mishra (a wheeling dealing lobbyist) squeezes her way towards Manav.

MALINI MISHRA *(To someone)*
Excuse me!...

MALINI MISHRA *(To someone)*
Excuse me!...

She grabs him by the collar and leads him away to some privacy. She literally pins him on the door to a private room. She doesn't miss a beat as she snuggles into Manav and grinding herself against him, she asks.

MALINI MISHRA *(To Manav)*
So! Have you thought about my offer?

MALINI MISHRA *(To Manav)*
So!... क्या सोचा मेरे Offer के बारे में?...

MALINI MISHRA
You know... Wishtel guys are here!

MALINI MISHRA
You know... Wishtel guys are here!

MALINI MISHRA *(contd)*
Ready with a Blank Cheque!!

MALINI MISHRA *(contd)*
Ready with a Blank Cheque!!

Manav looks impressed and smiles. But is of course not intersted...

MALINI MISHRA
Manav, why are you so stubborn! They are giving you such a good offer... 500 Million Dollars for 50% Stake...

MALINI MISHRA
मानव... तुम इतने ज़िद्दी क्यूँ हो?... They are giving you such a good offer... 500 Million Dollars for 50% Stake...

OFF SCREEN
600..

OFF SCREEN
600..

Manav looks at the two men who have appeared from nowhere. He looks back at Malini –

MALINI MISHRA
Rajat and Suri from Wishtel... Darling.. You know my connections in the private sector and in the Government are... much better than your Sundarlal Khatri. I can turn your FUTURE-V dream Project
(snaps her fingers)
into reality like that.

MALINI MISHRA
Rajat and Suri from Wishtel... Darling.. तुम्हें पता है... मेरे Private sector के Connections और Government Sector के भी, are much better than your Sundarlal Khatri... तुम्हारा FUTURE-V Project
(snaps her fingers)
यूँ Reality में बदल दूँगी...

Manav's eyes slip down to her cleavage. She is too close for comfort. He smiles at the men and then brushing her hair off her face with his fingers he flirts with her.

MANAV
The package isn't bad Ms. Malini Mishra. But, you see, until I finish playing with my dreams fully, I don't sell them.

MANAV
Package बुरा नहीं है Ms. Malini Mishra...लेकिन जब तक मैं अपने सपनों के साथ पूरी तरह खेल ना लूँ... उन्हें बेचता नहीं...

Manav walks away back onto the dance floor where the exotic dancer gyrates around him.

Sundarlal Khatri introduces Manav to H. Parekh (40, gold-rimmed spectacles, pencil-thin moustache, oozing that peculiar confidence that comes from having a mountain of cash at home)

SUNDARLAL KHATRI
My friend, for the last 3 years you've been waiting for the policy to change. In our system, unless you twist your finger, it doesn't happen.

SUNDARLAL KHATRI
My friend – आप पिछले तीन साल से Policy बदलने का इंतज़ार कर रहे हैं... अपने System में ये अपने आप नहीं होता – उँगली टेढ़ी करेंगे तभी घी निकलेगा –

ABP

BACK TO SCHOOL!

Kareena says shooting for Satyagraha was like being in boarding school. She had these long lines that she had to rattle in a fast paced 'reporter' rhythm. Not used to it, she would often stay up till the wee hours of the morning learning her lines!

Manav impassively gazes back at him..

SUNDARLAL KHATRI
And, I have brought you that finger! Meet H. Parekh.

SUNDARLAL KHATRI
In the market, he has a different name – C & C

MANAV
C&C?

H. Parekh laughs.

HARINATH
Cash and contacts! He keeps Rs. 400 billion in one pocket, and 150 MP's in the other.

SUNDARLAL KHATRI
And, ministers in his secret pocket! Including telecom. Got it?

H.PAREKH
I hear you're launching a new mobile soon – Future-IV. I'll get you both - investment and a change in policy. Win-win for both of us.

SUNDARLAL KHATRI
और मैं... उँगली को खुद लेकर आया हूँ... ये एच. पारेख हैं...

SUNDARLAL KHATRI
वैसे Market में इनका नाम अलग है – C&C..

MANAV
C&C?

HARINATH
Cash and Contacts!... इनके एक जेब में 40 हज़ार करोड़... और दूसरे में डेढ़ सौ M.P.

SUNDARLAL KHATRI
और Inside pocket में मंत्री... Including telecom!.. अब समझे?

H.PAREKH
सुना है – अपना नया Mobile Market में Launch करने वाले हो... FUTURE IV... मैं आपको Investments और Change in Policy दोनों दूँगा... Well.. Win Win for both of us..

They toast to the thought when suddenly a young lady Yasmin Ahmed accosts him purposefully, with the most false smile you could see.

The until-now-cool H.Parekh suddenly begins to fidget and stutter..

H.PAREKH
Oh.. Err.. Ms. Yasmin?

Yasmin continues the mock exaggerated courtesy..

YASMIN
When did you return from Singapore?

H.PAREKH
Singapore??

YASMIN
Yes, that's what I was told by your office. At 4 AM, you were in America. Next call, you were in France. London in the afternoon. And an hour ago? Singapore! Wow! You really move fast.

H.PAREKH
You.. you should've called me directly!

H.PAREKH
अरे, या... यास्मिन जी!

YASMIN
आप Singapore से कब लौटे?

H.PAREKH
Singapore??

YASMIN
हाँ!... यही तो कहा आपके Office ने... कि चार बजे सुबह आप America में थे... फिर France पहुँच गये... दोपहर को London में... और अब एक घंटे पहले, Singapore!... Wow, you really move fast –अँऽ...

H.PAREKH
आ... आप मुझे Direct phone कर लेतीं!

YASMIN
17 missed calls!

YASMIN
17 missed calls!

H.PAREKH *(actually smiling, smugly)*
I.. I keep busy. I'm very sorry.

H.PAREKH *(actually smiling, smugly)*
देखिए मैं कितना Busy हूँ... I'm very sorry..

YASMIN *(Seriously)*
You should apologise to yourself.

YASMIN *(Seriously)*
आप अपने आपको Sorry बोलिए...

He's surprised.

YASMIN
Excuse me!...

YASMIN
Excuse me!...

Yasmin takes out a tablet and holds it up for Mr. Parekh to see the news. On the tablet, a news anchor introduces Yasmin's story.

ANCHOR *(on Tablet)*
Breaking news: The latest report on H. Parekh..

ANCHOR *(on Tablet)*
Breaking News में... एच. पारेख पर File की गई ताज़ा Story -

YASMIN *(on Tablet)*
This is not merely about graft. The law and policy-making machinery of the country itself is being controlled!

YASMIN *(on Tablet)*
ये सिर्फ़ रिश्वत का मामला नहीं है... ये देश के कानून और Policy-making machinery को Control करने का खेल है!

In sting-operation-like grainy visuals, we can distinctly make out H.Parekh boasting to the Camera..

H.PAREKH *(on TV)*
Name it, and that policy can be changed. All you need is cash! Mining Regulations were changed thrice last year, weren't they? How?

H.PAREKH *(on TV)*
जो Policy बदलनी है, बदली जा सकती है... सिर्फ़ माल की ज़रूरत है, माल की... क्यों... पिछले साल Mining के Regulations तीन बार नहीं बदले?... कैसे?.. बदले ना...

YASMIN *(on TV)*
That was Mr. H. Parekh. Mumbai's biggest stock investor. Fondly known as C&C. Mr. Cash and Contacts!

YASMIN *(on TV)*
तो ये थे Mr. H.Parekh.. मुंबई के सबसे बड़े Stock Investor.. जिनको प्यार से Mr. C&C कहा जाता है. Mr. Cash and Contacts!

Sudarlal Khatri and H. Parekh leave but, Manav moves forward and holds out his hand..

MANAV
I'm a fan!... Love your reports..

MANAV
I'm a fan!... Love your reports..

She takes his hand, surprised. Then peers at him.. Meanwhile Hari, Manav's associate introduces him..

HARI
Yasmin, This is Manav.

HARI
Yasmin, This is Mr. Manav -

YASMIN
Raghvendra. The rising star of the Communication Sector..

YASMIN
राघवेन्द्र... The rising star of the communication sector..

YASMIN
I hope our paths don't cross..

YASMIN
I hope our paths don't cross..

MANAV
I hope they do!

MANAV
I hope they do!

Yasmin leaves.

INT/EXT DWARKA HOUSE - VERANDAHDAY

It is still early in the morning.. Sumitra hands the newspaper to Dwarka.

SUMITRA
Dad...

SUMITRA
बाबू जी...

DWARKA
Ah. Thank you. Thank you.

DWARKA
हाँ... आऽऽ Thank you – Thank you!

INT DWARKA HOUSE KITCHEN/DINING ROOM DAY

Sumitra rushes back to the kitchen where there is a flurry of activity.

SUMITRA
Open that packet of India Gate.

SUMITRA
अरे वो India Gate का Packet खोला?..

MAID
Yes.

MAID
जी...

SUMITRA *(soaks the rice)*
We need to cook the rice, right?

SUMITRA *(soaks the rice)*
चावल भिगोना पड़ेगा ना...

MAID
Yes.

MAID
जी...

Akhilesh says his morning prayers. But the hands kneading the flour conitnue –

SUMITRA
You peel the cabbage, while I will knead the dough.

SUMITRA
तू गोभी घिस, मैं लगाती हूँ आटा...

Sumitra starts taking out the flour to prepare it.

MAID
I'll do it, Madam.

MAID
मैं करती हूँ ना दीदी –

SUMITRA
Don't worry. I'm on it.

SUMITRA
अरे नहीं नहीं मैं करती हूँ –

Sumitra notices Akhilesh through the door. Her eyes catch Akhilesh getting ready, and as he picks up a shirt she almost screams –

SUMITRA
Not that one! The blue one. In the wardrobe.

SUMITRA
अरे अरे वो वाली नहीं – मैंने रखी है अलमारी में – Blue वाली Shirt -

Even as Sumitra walks in the room, her hands covered with flour Akhilesh looks baffled wondering what was wrong with the shirt he has picked up.

AKHILESH
What's wrong with this one?

AKHILESH
अरे इसमें क्या Problem है यार!

Sumitra has walked to the cupboard and is pointing to the blue shirt...

SUMITRA
Hang on a second. See? This one.

SUMITRA
ओहो... एक Minute.. देखो – ये वाली...

SUMITRA
Blue goes better with khaki trousers. C'mon.. Help me

SUMITRA
अरे, खाकी Pant के साथ Blue वाली अच्छी लगेगी... अरे Help ना, Come on..

Just then he spots her trying to pull the shirt, with her elbows, her back looking most inviting. Sneaks upto her and grabs her from behind.

Sumitra, startled shrieks and turns around, pasting his face with the flour.

SUMITRA
Gosh, what're are you doing?!

SUMITRA
अरे क्या कर रहे हो!

AKHILESH
Now, don't I have this freedom either?

AKHILESH
अब ये करने की भी आज़ादी नहीं है क्या?

SUMITRA
See what happened? You'll need to shower again.

SUMITRA
अब हो गया ना – अब वापस नहाना पड़ेगा...

He continues to hold her.

AKHILESH *(teasing)*
Join me, then.

AKHILESH *(teasing)*
चलो, नहला दो ना...

SUMITRA
You're incorrigible! Let go.

SUMITRA
तुम मानोगे नहीं ना – छोड़ो यार...

He pulls her closer..

MAID *(O.S)*
Ma'am, should I add the rice? The water is..

MAID (O.S)
दीदी, चावल डाल दूँ... पानी खौल –

And just then, the maid walks in and gasps and goes back embarassed. Akki rolls his eyes and releases her, as she giggles.

INT/EXT DWARKAS HOUSE VERANDAH DAY

Outside, Dwarka is busy with the newspaper which has the picture of a flyover and information about its inauguration in the headlines.

SUMITRA *(O.S)*
Breakfast is ready.

SUMITRA (O.S)
नाश्ता लग गया बाबूजी...

INT DWARKAS HOUSE DINING ROOM DAY

Dwarka walks in to sit down for breakfast.

DWARKA
Akhilesh...

DWARKA
अरे अखिलेश...

Akhilesh, buttoning his cuffs also heads to the breakfast table.

AKHILESH
Yes, father.

AKHILESH
जी, बाउजी...

DWARKA
Terrific design, Akhilesh! Project being completed in record time too! At this rate, we'll soon overtake Chinese efficiency.

DWARKA
बेटा क्या Design बनाया है तुमने... अँयँ!... Record Time में पूरा करने वाले हो इसे... इसी तरह काम करते रहे तो... China को पछाड़ देंगे हम लोग...

Dwarka and Akhilesh sit down at the breakfast table as Sumitra starts laying out the breakfast. Akhilesh does not look very enthusiastic in his response.

AKHILESH
There's pressure from Minister Balaram Singh.

AKHILESH
मंत्री बलराम सिंह का बड़ा दबाव है –

DWARKA
I see.

DWARKA
अच्छा!

AKHILESH
He wants to inaugurate it before the upcoming elections.

AKHILESH
Election के पहले ही Inaugurate करना चाहते हैं...

As Sumitra brings in the tray with rice and fresh Parathas and serves them, Akhilesh's phone rings..

DWARKA
Aha! Smells wonderful!
(takes a paratha)
Parathas! Which ones?

DWARKA
आऽऽ हाहाहा!!... क्या खुशबू आ रही है खाने की...
(takes a paratha)
लाओ लाओ लाओ – पराठा देओ... किस चीज़ का है – एँ...

SUMITRA
Cabbage parathas.

SUMITRA
गोभी के पराठे –

DWARKA
Excellent! And what is this? Grams.

DWARKA
अच्छा–अच्छा!... ये क्या बना है – ये चना है?...

AKHILESH *(answering the phone)*
Hello?

AKHILESH *(answering the phone)*
Hello?

SITE ENGINEER *(on phone)*
Sir, an entire slab of the flyover fell off.

SITE ENGINEER *(on phone)*
Sir, Flyover का Slab गिर गया है Sir..

At this news, Akhilesh stands up in shock. Both Sumitra and Dwarka are startled by Akhilesh's response on the phone.

AKHILESH *(on the phone)*
Oh God! When?

AKHILESH *(on the phone)*
Oh God! कब हुआ ये!?

SITE ENGINEER *(on the phone)*
Just now, Sir. 7 to 8 people were badly crushed, sir.

SITE ENGINEER *(on the phone)*
बस, अभी थोड़ी देर पहले Sir- सात–आठ मजदूर दब गये हैं, Sir...

AKHILESH *(on the phone)*
Call an Ambulance.

AKHILESH *(on the phone)*
Ambulance बुलाओ –

SITE ENGINEER *(on phone)*
Yes Sir.

SITE ENGINEER *(on phone)*
जी Sir..

As Akhilesh hangs up the phone, Dwarka gets up and asks Akhilesh what the matter is.

DWARKA
What happened, son?

DWARKA
क्या बात है बेटा?

AKHILESH
A slab from the flyover collapsed.

AKHILESH
Flyover का एक Slab गिर गया बाबूजी...

DWARKA
Oh God!

DWARKA
हे भगवान्!...

SUMITRA
What?!

SUMITRA
What?!

DWARKA
Any casualties?

DWARKA
कोई बड़ी दुर्घटना तो नहीं हुई?...

AKHILESH
Some workers, perhaps.

AKHILESH
कुछ मजदूर शायद...

Sumitra too looks worried.

INT/EXT DWARKAS HOUSE DAY

Akhilesh pulls out his motorbyke and zooms off even as his father and wife look worried.

SITE OF THE FLYOVER – EXT : MORNING/DAY

Arjun Rajvanshi, a local leader who is trying to make it in Politics, arrives at the site, The flyover has fallen and many people have been injured and are caught underneath the debris.

ARJUN
Stop the car! Step back. Step back everyone! Shift the injured in our cars and take them to the hospital. Quickly.

ARJUN
रुक रुक रुक... अरे गाड़ी रोक... पीछे हटाओ सबको... जल्दी–जल्दी... पीछे हटाओ... ए... जो घायल हैं सबको गाड़ी में लेके चल... चल, जल्दी – जल्दी Hospital लेके चल...

Autograph please!

When some kids asked for Amrita Rao's autograph, as a joke Mr. Bachchan signed for her. Amrita was shocked and supremely delighted to note that his signature was very similar to her own! She now has her own autograph by Mr. Bachchan framed and occupying pride of place in her house.

As Akhilesh arrives, Arjun shows him the sire and Akhilesh is very disturbed. He sees the bodies being taken away, the injured in pain. Looks at the broken part of the bridge. He picks up some stray cement and examines it with an angry grimace.

ARJUN
Look at that...

ARJUN
वो देख...

AKHILESH
I had issued written instructions to use only Ultratech Cement! But, they used inferior stuff.

AKHILESH
लिख कर दिया था मैंने कि सिर्फ़ Ultra Tech Cement लगायें... लेकिन... घटिया माल इस्तेमाल किया है!

AKHILESH *[contd.] (Really angry now)*
I'm going to get to the bloody bottom of this!

AKHILESH *[contd.] (Really angry now)*
I'm going to get to the bloody bottom of this!

ARJUN
You do that, Akhilesh. And let me know. We won't spare anyone, no matter what.

ARJUN
पता लगाओ, अखिलेश, और बताओ हमको... हम छोड़ेंगे नहीं... चाहे कुछ भी हो जाए –

It is at this moment that Gauri Shankar the leader of the opposition and his men arrive with a bunch of media.

Arjun reacts to this with disgust.

ARJUN
Here he comes! To play politics with the dead.

ARJUN
लो... आ गया ये... लाशों पे राजनीति करने –

MEDIA
Mr. Gauri Shankar, you are the Leader of the Opposition. Are you going to demand for their resignation?

MEDIA
गौरी शंकर जी, आप Opposition के Leader हैं – तो क्या आप उनके इस्तीफ़े की माँग करेंगे?...

GAURI SHANKAR
I will. But, to what end? This government stands on the crutches of Balram Singh's 8 legislators. Remove those, and it collapses.

GAURI SHANKAR
करेंगे! लेकिन फ़ायदा क्या!... बलराम सिंह के आठ विधायकों की बैसाखी पे खड़ी है ये सरकार... वो गये... तो ये गिरे...

MEDIA-2
But sir, you are in the Road and Bridge Construction Committee.

MEDIA-2
लेकिन Sir, सरकार की सड़क और पुल निर्माण Committee के Member तो आप भी हैं...

GAURI SHANKAR
I will make them account for every single life buried beneath this corruption. Balram Singh has crossed all limits.

GAURI SHANKAR
लेकिन, मैं इस भ्रष्टाचार के तले कुचली एक–एक जान का हिसाब लूँगा... Limit की भी Limit Cross कर चुका है बलराम सिंह...

EXT SECRETARIAT DAY

A cavalcade of cars enter the secretariat.

BALRAM SINGH *(O.S.) (Laughs)*
Hah! You make it sound like this is the first time a Flyover has collapsed in India!....

BALRAM SINGH(O.S.) *(Laughs)*
अरे... अरे भाई, आप लोग तो ऐसे बात कर रहे हैं... जैसे India में First Time कोई Flyover गिरा है... उँ...

INT CABINET COMMITTEE HALL DAY

Great Fireworks! The opposition leader Gauri Shankar, the C.M., Kalikant Babu are all there at the Committee meeting..

BALRAM SINGH *(contd)*
The family of every worker killed was given Rs. 100,000! And, the injured Rs. 50,000! Within 24 hours!! We've set up 3 Expert Committees and Consultants to investigate the accident. Read the report carefully. Go on! To prevent such mishaps, we need strong and modern technology. The cost will shoot up. Even a villager understands: You want top quality, shell out top dollar!

BALRAM SINGH *(contd)*
मरे हुए लोगों को One Lac Rupees each और घायलों को Fifty Thousand rupees each - Twenty four hour के अन्दर Sanction कर दिया है... तीन–तीन Expert Committee और Consultant से Examine करवा रहे हैं हम – ध्यान से पढ़िए Report आप लोग... पढ़िए–पढ़िए... और भविष्य में ऐसा हादसा ना हो इसके लिए Design में Strong और Modern Technology का इस्तेमाल करना पड़ेगा... Cost बढ़ेगा... और ये तो Village का आदमी भी जानता है कि माल चाहिए चोखा... तो नोट करो जी मोटा... हें!...

KALIKANT BABU
Next proposal?

KALIKANT BABU
अगला प्रस्ताव क्या है?

THE LADY,CABINET MAMEBER
National Highway 4.

THE LADY,CABINET MAMEBER
N.H.4...

THE MINISTER
Rs. 5.73 billion.

THE MINISTER
573 करोड़... क्या भाई?

C.M.
Passed!

C.M.
पारित किया जाता है –

INT CABINET COMMITTEE HALL LATER

Gauri Shankar picks up a handful of Cashew-nuts and talks to Balram Singh privately.

GAURI SHANKAR
What is this, Balram Sir! Not only do you not clear my Tikari Bridge contract..

GAURI SHANKAR
क्या बलराम बाबू... एक तो आप हमारा Tikari Bridge का जो Contract Pass नहीं कर रहे और दूसरा वो –

BALRAM SINGH
Chill, pal. I'll get it done. Tikari has been reserved for you.

BALRAM SINGH
अरे करवा देंगे ना भाई... करवा देंगे ना... आप ही के लिए तो रखा है Tikari -

GAURI SHANKAR
And, cost escalation? For both projects, only 70%?!

GAURI SHANKAR
Rate Revision – दो चालू Project हैं... सिर्फ़ सत्तर Percent देख लीजिए आप –

BALRAM SINGH
The CM vetoed it! Flatly refused to go beyond 50%.

BALRAM SINGH
अरे Veto लगा दिये हैं C.M.... वो Fifty percent से ज्यादे के लिए तैयार ही नहीं थे...

Gauri Shankar gives a dirty look to the C.M.

GAURI SHANKAR
Glory be to the old man! His relatives have hijacked the Mid Day Meal Scheme, PDS and even the 4-lane highway. What's left for us? Squat!

BALRAM SINGH
You need to work harder, sir. Manage the numbers in the next election. I'll adjust with you. Then everything's yours – PDS, Mid-Day 4-lane, flyover. Anything and everything!!

GAURI SHANKAR
धन्य है बुढ़ऊ!... Mid Day Scheme का जो Meal का Scheme है... पूरा खा गया इसका साला... P.D.S. ले उड़ा इसका बहनोई – अब Four Lane भी... हम लोग के लिए क्या बचेगा – घंटा!

BALRAM SINGH
मेहनत कीजिए ना Sir... अगला चुनाव में आप जुगाड़ कर लीजिए Number... फिर हम साला आपके साथ Adjust हो जायेंगे... और आप Filter करते रहिए... P.D.S., Mid Day, Four Lane – Fly over – Anything and Everything!!...हुम्म... मेवा खाइए!...

Gauri Shankar's bitter frustration is evident..

COMMUNITY CENTRE – EXT: DAY

MANAV
How are you, Sumi?

MANAV
कैसी हो, सुमी?

SUMITRA
Pulling along.. And, you?

SUMITRA
बस... आप बताइये –

MANAV
Is Akki okay?

MANAV
अक्की ठीक है?

She hesitates...

SUMITRA
Yes, why?

SUMITRA
हाँ... क्यों?

MANAV
I've been calling him all afternoon.. He won't answer the phone.

MANAV
दोपहर से Phone कर रहा हूँ – Phone नहीं उठा रहा है...

SUMITRA
He's been a bit disturbed since the flyover accident.

SUMITRA
हाँऽऽ... वो जब से Flyover का Accident हुआ है ना भइया... थोड़े Disturbed रहते हैं...

MANAV
But, that wasn't his fault!

MANAV
अरे कितनी बार समझा चुका हूँ कि उसकी ग़लती नहीं है –

SUMITRA
Well, but you know how he is.. He feels responsible for it.

SUMITRA
हाँ, पर आप जानते हैं ना... खुद की Responsibility मान बैठे हैं...

MANAV
Do get him to call me. You guys need a break.

MANAV
आये तो Phone करवाना... You guys need a break..

Sumitra laughs –

SUMITRA
I know...

SUMITRA
I know...

MANAV
Uncle okay?

MANAV
Uncle ठीक हैं?

SUMITRA
Yes, busy teaching. And venting his anger on everything that is wrong with the world.

SUMITRA
बस, लगे रहते हैं पढ़ाने में... और दुनिया में जो भी ग़लत हो रहा है – उस पर गुस्सा निकालने में...

Manav laughs -

MANAV
Ok, Bye...

MANAV
Ok, Bye...

MAIN ROAD / HIGHWAY – EXT: DAY

Akhilesh is driving his bike back home – Sumitra dials his number but he doesn't hear his phone ringing.

It's a relatively empty part of the highway. A truck closes in on him. The motorcycle driving ahead dangerously sways and skids on some dirt as it is overloaded with cans of diesel and mobil oil. Akhilesh's bike looses balance and skids on the oil spill, crashing on the road.

The truck runs over Akhilesh. The tyres of the truck pass inches close to the guy on the bike with oil, who escapes miraculously. He sees the truck run over Akhilesh and is left in shock.

HOSPITAL CORRIDOR – INT: DAY

Sumitra's on the phone with Manav. She breaks down!

SUMITRA
Manav bhaiya... Akhilesh...

SUMITRA
भइया... मानव भइया... अखिलेश...

In her background we see a stunned Dwarka looking as Akhilesh's body is wheeled out of the operation theatre.

Some where close by Durgalal, the Kotwali Police Inspector is briefing Media men..

DURGALAL *(Pointing to a bruised man)*
His name is Chhotelal. Still traumatised. He sells diesel in the villages. His bike skidded; Akhilesh Anand's bike behind him also skidded. There was a truck behind him. That's it. The truck driver is absconding. We're investigating further.

DURGALAL *(Pointing to a bruised man)*
छोटेलाल नाम है इसका... अभी सदमे में है... Diesel Oil बेचता है गाँव के बाज़ार में... Skid कर गया वहीं पे... पीछे से अखिलेश आनन्द की Bike आ रही थी... वो भी Skid कर गया... Truck आ रहा था पीछे से... बस... Truck Driver फ़रार है... हम लोग बाकी की Investigation कर रहे हैं...

DWARKA HOUSE – EXT/INT :DAY

As Manav arrives, Akhilesh's body is laid outside... Dwarka's calm demeanour is failing to cover the grief he is going through... The moment Sumitra spots Manav getting off from the car, she begins to howl and comes to Manav. He holds her protectively, trying to fight his own tears as she bawls openly..

SUMITRA
He's gone! What'll become of us now?

SUMITRA
वो चला गया... अब हमारा क्या होगा!!!...

Manav stares at Akhilesh's body.

Over her head, he looks at Dwarka, who stares back with vacant eyes.

The Pandit gestures to Dwarka that they should be moving to the cremation ground.

PANDIT
It's time, sir..

PANDIT
चलने का समय हो गया है यजमान...

Everyone there looks surprised as jeeps with cops arrive along with media persons on motorcycles. Manav looks on as he hears the blaring sirens of a minister's cavalcade led by the District Collector. The D.M. walks up to Dwarka-

D.M.
I am B.K. Prasad, the District Magistrate. Minister Balram Singh is here.

D.M.
मैं बी. के. प्रसाद... यहाँ का D.M. ... मंत्री बलराम सिंह जी आये हैं...

Dwarka looks at the Minister who emerges from his car and places a wreath on Akhilesh's body.

The Minister walks up to Dwarka and offers his condolences.

BALRAM SINGH
There cannot be any greater pain for a father.. Such a terrible shock!

BALRAM SINGH
एक Father के लिए... इससे बड़ा संताप कुछ हो ही नहीं सकता... बहुत बड़ा सदमा है ये...

He moves on and addresses the media.

BALRAM SINGH
Akhilesh Anand was a top class Gold Medalist! A superb engineer. I was looking to him for the development of this district. Nothing can bring him back, of course.. But, as a small token of compensation I announce a sum Rs. 2.5 million.

BALRAM SINGH
Top Class, Gold Medalist थे अखिलेश आनन्द... इतना बढ़िया Engineer, अपने ज़िला के विकास के लिए कितना भरोसा करके हम बैठे थे... कोई भी कीमत उनको वापस लौटा के नहीं दे सकती... पर सरकार की तरफ़ से एक तुच्छ भेंट के रूप में पच्चिस लाख का Payment हम Announce करते हैं –

BULBUL SINGH
Wonderful! Wonderful! This is great!

BULBUL SINGH
वाह् वाह्... बहुत अच्छे... बधाई हो – बधाई हो... वाह् वाह्...

Bulbul Singh, like a fool, claps and starts singing praises until Balram looks back sharply at him, and he stops, sheepishly.

BALRAM SINGH *(To Bulbul)*
गधा है...
(To himself)
Oh God!

BALRAM SINGH *(To Bulbul)*
गधा है...
(To himself)
हे भगवान्...

Manav looks on with tears in his eyes.

DWARKA HOUSE – INT/ TERRACE: NIGHT

Dwarka is sitting on his bed, staring at the floor. He hears Sumitra crying.

He goes to Sumitra's room. She is lying on her bed and crying. He fixes the sheet on her and places his hand on her head.

Dwarka walks up the stairs and finds Manav standing, bent over, with his hands on the parapet. Still. At the same spot where Dwarka had seen him last when the two had a massive showdown. Manav hasn't heard Dwarka come up. Dwarka is a bit taken aback to see him like this, and stands for a moment to watch.

And then, Manav turns his head, and spots the flask that Akki had hastily hidden the night they were drinking here.

The sight of the flask makes Manav break down. He sits down to control himself, but is unable to. It is like his whole body cracks up, in huge heaving sobs.

Dwarka watches.

And then, he quietly turns around and goes away.

EXT. HIGHWAY: MORNING/EVENING

Manav driving – Comes across a massive Blockade – Huge Police Barricades – Private cars told to turn back and take another route-

A COP Please go back. This road's closed. There's a diversion there.. C'mon.. Please take that..	**A COP** चलिए Return होइए... यहाँ Road block है... Back होइए... Diversion है पीछे... चलिए... वहाँ से मुड़ जाइए...

Manav gets off his car, walks to the Blockade to find out the reason- Comes accross thousands of people who have been stopped over the bridge – Sees Banners reading SATYAGRAH MARCH TO DELHI... IT IS OUR LAND! WE DON'T WANT TO GIVE IT UP! ETC.. Looks at an officer –

MANAV What's going on?	**MANAV** क्या हो रहा है?
POLICE OFFICER They're agitating for land, sir. Plan was to march all the way to Delhi. But, orders are to stop them here.	**POLICE OFFICER** ज़मीन के लिए लड़ रहे हैं Sir... दिल्ली तक Marching का Programme था – अब यहीं रोक देने का Order हुआ है...
MANAV How long will they sit here for?	**MANAV** कब तक बैठेंगे?
POLICE OFFICER Oh, these guys are very stubborn! They can hold out for days on end.	**POLICE OFFICER** ये साहब बड़े ढीठ लोग हैं – कई–कई दिन डेरा डाल देते हैं –

Manav nods and turns to leave when he hears a voice- He seems to recognise the voice..

YASMIN On whose orders have you closed this road? Why can't I go in? *(shows her batch)* Look here, I'm the Chief Correspondent of..	**YASMIN** किसकी Authority से आपने इनका रास्ता रोक रखा है – और मुझे क्यूँ नहीं जाने दे रहे आप... *(shows her batch)* ये देखिए... Chief Correspondent हूँ मैं –

YASMIN *[contd.]*
...ABP News Channel. Yasmin Ahmed. You can't do this to me! I've come from Delhi to cover this.

YASMIN *[contd.]*
ABP News Channel... Yasmin Ahmed.. You can't do this to me... इनकी Story करने मैं दिल्ली से आई हूँ –

Manav turns to watch her and looks amazed at this fiesty woman fighting with the Cop – The Cop tells her...

POLICE OFFICER
Sorry, madam, the area beyond the barricade is restricted.

POLICE OFFICER
Sorry, Madam, Barricade के आगे का Area Restricted है –

YASMIN
How can you do this! Thousands of poor laborers have been fighting for their land for years. No one wants to even listen to them?! Let them reach Delhi, so this deaf government can hear them!

YASMIN
ये कोई तरीका है... हज़ारों ग़रीब मजदूर सालों से अपनी ज़मीन के लिए तरस रहे हैं... और कोई सुनता ही नहीं... पहुँचने दीजिए इनको दिल्ली तक... ताकि बहरी सरकार सुने इनको!

POLICE OFFICER
Sorry, Ma'am!...

POLICE OFFICER
Sorry, Ma'am!...

As the officer turns away, she notices Manav looking at her – Is surprised..

YASMIN
You? What're you doing here?

YASMIN
आप?... आप यहाँ पे क्या कर रहे हैं?

Manav shrugs...

MANAV
Don't know...

MANAV
पता नहीं...

YASMIN
But, where were you going?

YASMIN
लेकिन जा कहाँ रहे हैं?

MANAV
I really don't know...

MANAV
I really don't know...

YASMIN *(concerned)*
Are you okay?

YASMIN *(concerned)*
Are you okay?

He just looks down, unresponsive and reflective.

She notices the Tea shop next to the road...

YASMIN
How about a cup of tea?

YASMIN
चाय पियें?

INT. BASIC CHAI SHOP: DAY

They sit at a makeshift Tea shop against the backdrop of the protest –

She is looking at him moved, as he has just told her about Akhilesh's sudden death..

YASMIN *(Struggling for words)*
He was your brother!

YASMIN *(Struggling for words)*
भाई था वो तुम्हारा!!

MANAV
Technically, no. But, he was much more than that. I lost my parents in a terrible accident. If Akhilesh wasn't there, I would've fallen apart. And today, he has orphaned me again! Anyway, let it be.. lest I break down again.

MANAV
Technically नहीं... लेकिन उससे भी बढ़ कर... I Lost my Mom and Dad in a terrible accident... तब अखिलेश ने ही मुझे टूटने से बचाया... वो नहीं होता तो... और आज दुबारा मुझे अनाथ बना कर चला गया... चलो छोड़ो इस Topic को... सम्हालना मुश्किल हो जाएगा...

He is getting overcome again, and regains his composure.

He stands up asks-

MANAV
Can I drop you somewhere?

MANAV
कहीं छोड़ दूँ...

YASMIN
Where are you going?

YASMIN
तुम जा कहाँ रहे हो?...

MANAV
Told you. Just driving around.

MANAV
Told you. Just driving around.

YASMIN
I wish I could just drive around. But I have to cover this protest.

YASMIN
I'd love to do that, just drive around.. पर मुझे इस Protest की Story करनी है...

He looks towards the barricades.

MANAV
Let me try. Only for you.

MANAV
Let me try. Only for you.

He walks up to the officers and we don't really see what he has done or said. The officer relents and Manav signals for Yasmin to cross over.

She smiles and looks at him -

YASMIN
I know what you did.

YASMIN
मैं जानती हूँ तुमने क्या किया?

MANAV
Needs to be done. For a cause.

MANAV
करना पड़ता है... For a cause...

YASMIN
This time it's okay.

YASMIN
This time it's okay.

Manav smiles.. Watches her walk towards the protestors.

What a treat!

The icecreamwala, thelawalas and chaatwalas were thrilled to set up shop in Gandhi Chowk and be part of the film set. And they would happily treat the crew to free chaats and ice cream all day!

The D.M. continues-

D.M.
I told you you'll get the money. Now, should I construct a martyr's memorial as well?

D.M.
बोल तो दिये दे देंगे पैसा... अब क्या शहीद स्मारक बनवा दें...

DWARKA
Enough!!!

DWARKA
बस!!!...

The sudden sound of a TIGHT SLAP brings everything to halt... The D.M. is stunned and so are the committee members –

DWARKA
Enough! You are a public servant! And, we shall not tolerate your rudeness!

DWARKA
Enough!... नौकर हैं आप जनता के... और बद्तमीज़ी बर्दाश्त नहीं करेंगे हम...

The D.M. screams at his armed guards who have rushed into the room –

D.M.
Arrest him! Arrest him. Take him away.

D.M.
Arrest करो इनको... Arrest करो... लेके जाओ... लेके जाओ यहाँ से...

DWARKA
Hands off!

DWARKA
छोड़िए...

D.M.
Take him away!

D.M.
निकलिए बाहर...

DWARKA
I am going.

DWARKA
जा रहे हैं...

KOTWALI – EXT/INT: DAY

Arjun with some of his men storms into the Police Station –

ARJUN
What kind of justice is this, I ask?

ARJUN
ये कहाँ का न्याय है हम पूछते हैं...

The Senior Inspector asks him to calm down-

Sr.INSP.DURGALAL
Calm down. This is a police station.

Sr.INSP.DURGALAL
अरे भाई शांत रहिए – ये कोतवाली थाना है...

Arjun walks up to Dwarka –

ARJUN
Sir, don't you worry. We will fight for you.

ARJUN
Sir... Sir, आप चिन्ता मत कीजिए – हम लड़ेंगे आपके लिए...

Dwarka looks blank, completely unimpressed...

ARJUN
I'm Arjun, sir. I studied under you..

ARJUN
मैं अर्जुन Sir- आपके School में –

DWARKA
Arjun Rajvansh! 15 years ago, I expelled you for hooliganism.

DWARKA
अर्जुन राजवंश सिंह... पन्द्रह वर्षों पहले गुण्डागर्दी के आरोप में आपको School से निकाल दिया था मैंने...

ARJUN
But, sir, now I'm a social worker.

ARJUN
लेकिन Sir, अब हम जनता की...

DWARKA
Thank you for coming. You may go now. I don't want your help.

DWARKA
धन्यवाद, धन्यवाद!... आप आये – अच्छा लगा... अब आप जायें... मुझे आपकी मदद नहीं चाहिए...

MANAV's OFFICE – EXT/INT: DAY

Manav is in the office in discussion with the staff..

His secretary comes in...

NANCY
Sir, it's Ms. Sumitra.

NANCY
Sir, सुमित्रा जी –

Manav takes the receiver–

Sumitra breaks down on the other side –

MANAV
Yes, Sumi..

MANAV
हाँ सुमी...

SUMITRA
Dad's been arrested!

SUMITRA
मानव भैया... Police ने बाबूजी को Arrest कर लिया है...

ON THE CAR/ DELHI: DAY

As a worried Manav heads to the Airport, he's speaking to Sunderlal Khatri-

KHATRI
It's a delicate situation, Manav. The Ambikapur collector is the Home Minister's key man. I do know the state's Finance Minister, Kalikant Choudhary. But, he's a straight guy, y'know..

KHATRI
मामला Touchy है, मानव... अम्बिकापुर का D.M., Home Minister का ख़ास आदमी है – वैसे उस State के Finance Minister कालिकांत चौधरी को जानता हूँ... लेकिन वो थोड़े से Straight किस्म के हैं...

MANAV
I understand, thanks.

MANAV
I understand, thanks.

SADAR POLICE STATION – EXT/INT : DAY

Manav's car arrives at the Police Station. A bunch of Senior lawyers from the city led by Indrojeet Sen are with him – Sumitra meets him in the corridor–

SUMITRA
The court has ordered police custody for 7 days.

SUMITRA
Court ने सात दिनों की Police custody दी है...

Manav spots Dwarka in the lock-up. Sitting on the floor with a bunch of other convicts, Dwarka is clamly reading a Newspaper... He looks up at Manav but his face remains expressionless.

Senior Lawyer Indrojeet Sen has been talking to Sr. Insp. Durgalal..

DURGALAL
Along with section 353, he's also charged under 120B. Bail might be tough.

DURGALAL
353 के साथ 120B भी लगाया है... Bail होनी मुश्किल हो जाएगी...

Indrojeet suggests –

INDROJEET SEN
There's just one option now. If the Collector himself withdraws his complaint..

INDROJEET SEN
बस अब एक ही उपाय है... Collector अगर अपनी Complain खुद से वापस ले तो... ये Letter है...

Manav looks at Dwarka and decides to talk to him-

He shows him the apology letter.

MANAV
Uncle..

MANAV
बाउ जी...

Dwarka looks at the letter and turns away.

He turns back and asks Manav-

DWARKA
What should I apologize for?

DWARKA
किस बात की माफ़ी लिख के दूँ इन्हें...

MANAV
I know that you have done no wrong. But, right now..

MANAV
मैं जानता हूँ आपने कोई ग़लती नहीं की... लेकिन इस वक़्त यहाँ से –

DWARKA
You know nothing! It's people like you who are primarily responsible for corrupting this system. I don't want any help from you.

DWARKA
कुछ नहीं जानते हैं आप... इस व्यवस्था को इस भ्रष्ट हालात तक पहुँचाने में... आप जैसे लोगों का भी... बड़ा हाथ है मानव जी... कोई मदद नहीं चाहिए मुझे आपसे...

MANAV
But, I need your help! I can't see you like this.

MANAV
लेकिन मुझे चाहिए आपकी मदद... मैं नहीं देख सकता आपको इन हालात में...

DWARKA
Don't bother about me. I can face this punishment.

DWARKA
मेरी चिन्ता मत कीजिए आप... अपनी सज़ा खुद भुगत सकता हूँ मैं...

Manav is helpless.

BARFI!
आनंद
रिहा करो

HOUSEFULL!

Arjun Rampal observed with some amusement that the cinema hall in Gandhi Chowk had a new UTV release every few days with posters being changed enthusiastically. And, he notes, they were always running house full!

D.M.'s OFFICE – EXT/INT : DAY

Indrojeet pleads with the D.M.-

INDROJEET SEN
Please forget what happened, sir. He was very disturbed then.

INDROJEET SEN
अब जो हो गया उसे भूल जाइए Sir... उनकी मानसिक हालत ठीक नहीं थी उस वक़्त...

D.M.
A few days in jail will set right every disturbance.

D.M.
कुछ दिन अन्दर रहेंगे... तो दिमाग बिलकुल ठीक हो जायेगा –

Indrojeet looks helpless. Manav takes over-

MANAV
Sir, I agree that you have been insulted. While it can't be reversed, you can be compensated.

MANAV
Sir, मैं मानता हूँ आपके साथ ज़्यादती हुई है... उसे Reverse तो नहीं पर... Compensate ज़रूर किया जा सकता है...

The D.M.'s eyebrows curl -

D.M.
What do you mean?

D.M.
आपका मतलब?

Manav blurts out -

MANAV
Whatever you want. Just name a figure.

MANAV
आप जो भी चाहें... बस आप मुँह खोलिए...

The D.M. is suddenly angry and gets up –

D.M.
So, you've come to buy me, have you? Get up and out! In two minutes, I'll have you arrested as well. Get out!!

D.M.
तो आप हमें खरीदने आये हैं... Get up and out... समझ क्या रखा है आपने... दो Minute में अन्दर हो जायेंगे आप भी – GET OUT!!..

INDROJEET SEN
Sir, we didn't mean..

INDROJEET SEN
Sir, हमारे कहने का मतलब –

D.M.
OUT!!... OUT!!!...

D.M.
OUT!!... OUT!!!...

Manav looks at him..

Hearing him shout, the doorman and security have come in –

Manav and Indrojeet Sen are already coming out. The lawyer looks a bit hassled..

Rumour quickly spreads that someone has again slapped the D.M.. By the time Manav is out in the corridor, there is a small crowd that has gathered out of curiosity-

Someone asks-

OFF SCREEN VOICE-MALE
Who slapped him?

OFF SCREEN VOICE-MALE
अरे, आज किसने मारा?!...

The Doorman is irritated-

DOORMAN
What nonsense are you asking. Move out of here. Clear off, now!
Someone says-
He's corrupt himself and now pretending to be such a gentleman...

DOORMAN
अरे क्या मारा–मारा... किसको मारा?... चलो हटो यहाँ से – भीड़ हटाओ...
Someone says-
"अरे घूस खाते हैं और बनते हैं Gentleman..."

Manav listens in as he walks out-

OLD MAN
These people understand just one language! Only Dwarka's slap will bring them to their senses.

OLD MAN
सुनेगा भाई – ये लोग अब बस एक ही जबान सुनेगा – द्वारका बाबू का थप्पड़ ही होश में लायेगा इनको...

CROWD GUY 2
THWACK!! Dwarka's slap turned his cheek red!

CROWD GUY 2
चटाक्!!! गाल लाल कर दिए थे मास्टर साहेब!

INDROJEET SEN
That's how it is here. Everyone's had it with them.

INDROJEET SEN
यहाँ ये हाल है Mr. Manav... सब त्रस्त हैं –

Manav is thinking..

DTP SHOP/ GHANDHI CHOWK – EXT/INT : DAY

Indrojeet Sen's car followed by a dozen kids on their motorbikes stops outside the DTP shop at Gandhi Chowk-Crouching behind a computer in a shop, Manav has finished designing a Poster – Dwarka's face behind Bars with the bold lines at the Bottom –

"Does this man deserve to be in jail?
If you want to change the System, come to Gandhi Chowk at 10 am."

"इस आदमी को क्या सलाखों के पीछे होना चाहिए??
System बदलना है तो गाँधी चौक आयें– सुबह 10 बजे।"

Indrojeet Sen introduces him to the young college kids –

INDROJEET SEN *(To kids)*
Do come!
(To Manav)
Hello..

INDROJEET SEN *(To kids)*
आ जाओ...
(To Manav)
Hello..

MANAV
Hi..

MANAV
Hi..

INDROJEET SEN
These are my son's college friends. For some loose change, they'll do the job...

INDROJEET SEN
ये सब College friends हैं हमारे बेटे के... थोड़ा बहुत Pocket money मिल जाये तो... कर देंगे आपका काम...

(to kids)
Right?

(To kids)
है कि नहीं...

VIPUL
Yes. It'll be done.

VIPUL
जी, बिल्कुल...

Manav picks up a stack of posters and hands them to the kids.

They look at the Poster..

MANAV
Put these up wherever you can... lanes, bylanes, crossroads..

MANAV
हर गली–नुक्कड़–चौराहे–बाज़ार... जहाँ भी लोगों का आना–जाना हो... ये चिपका दो...

One of the kids says-

VIPUL *(To another boy)*
By morning you'll see them everywhere.

VIPUL *(To another boy)*
कल सुबह हर जगह दिखेगा आपको...

He takes out a wad of notes and hands the money over. The kids pocket the money, sheepishly.

To another bunch of geeky looking kids, Manav shows a video. Its a cartoon of Dwarka slapping the D.M. with the caption –
The system is rotten. It needs to be cleaned up. Like this!

And as the slap comes on the D.M.'s face -
If you want to change the system, come to Gandhi Chowk at 10 am. We will fight together.

To another bunch of geeky looking kids, Manav shows a video. Its a cartoon of Dwarka slapping the D.M. with the caption –
"System सड़ गया है उसको साफ़ करना होगा... ऐसे!"

And as the slap comes on the D.M.'s face -
"अगर आप System बदलना चाहते हैं तो सुबह 10 बजे गाँधी चौक पर आइए... हम मिल कर लड़ेंगे –We will fight."

Indrojeet Sen hands over a stack of paper to the boys -

INDROJEET SEN
These are the numbers of all the mobile operators.

INDROJEET SEN
ये रहे सभी Mobile Operators के Numbers...

Manav tells the kids..

MANAV
Split these into batches of 10, and bombard them with the MMS.

MANAV
इसके दस–दस नम्बरों के Batch बनाओ... और भेजते रहो इस MMS को...

The kids look excited –

KIDS
Will be done, sir.

KIDS
हो जायेगा मानव भइया!

Manav tells Indrojeet Sen –

MANAV
Thank you Indrojeet. I know that you're a big lawyer..

MANAV
Thank you इन्द्रजीत... मुझे पता है आप इस शहर के बहुत बड़े Lawyer हैं–

INDROJEET SEN
Not at all Mr. Manav... I also have another name here: The proletariat lawyer!

INDROJEET SEN
Not at all Mr. Manav... शायद आपको ये नहीं मालूम कि इस शहर में मेरा और भी एक नाम है... रिक्शा और ठेला वकील!...

A couple of rickshaw drivers greet Indrojeet.

Manav laughs-

MANAV
How come?

MANAV
क्यूँ?...

INDROJEET SEN
I fight their cases free of cost. But from big shots and companies, I charge a bomb.

INDROJEET SEN
Free में लड़ता हूँ ना उनके Cases!... लेकिन बड़े लोगों और Companies के मामलों में तगड़ी फीस लेता हूँ –

Manav is impressed –

MANAV
Way to go, Man!

MANAV
Way to go, Man!

MONTAGE– EXT/INT: DAY

Kids paste posters on walls asking for Dwarka's release and questioning his action.

Manav takes them in a corner at Gandhi Chowk where some of the posters have been stuck on the walls and taking tight shots of the kids he makes them shout slogans –
"Release Dwarka Anand!"
"Every blow deserves a whack. Every corrupt man, deserves a slap."

"द्वारका आनन्द को रिहा करो..."
"ईंट का जवाब पत्थर से – भ्रष्टाचार का थप्पड़ से..."

He uses different backgrounds and tight shots..

MANAV
That's it. Change position. Those in front, move back.

MANAV
बस–बस... Position change करो... पीछे वाले आगे... आगे वाले पीछे...

Montage continues. Manav captures kids lighting candles at Dwarka's release poster at Gandhi Chowk. Kids spread the message on social media.

D.M. HOUSE – EXT/INT: DAY

The D.M. is getting ready at his residence when his phone beeps announcing a message – He clicks it on. The MMS plays as soon as it is loaded and the slap with its sound stings the D.M. His face turns white... The Audio asking people to collect at Gandhi Chowk stuns him...

GANDHI CHOWK – EXT : DAY

4-5 jeeps with Arjun and his men head towards Gandhi Chowk. It looks jammed – Arjun is surprised and asks one of the bystanders –

ARJUN
Hey Buddhan, what's going on here?

ARJUN
ए बुद्धन... ये क्या हो रहा है?

BUDDHAN
I don't know, looks like some new leader..

BUDDHAN
मालुम नहीं भैया, कोई नया नेता आया है–

ARJUN
New leader?! What the hell!

ARJUN
नया नेता?... ये कौन नौटंकी है स्साला –

Arjun gets off his vehicle and his men gather, looking excited for some action-

Manav is struggling with his speech trying to enthuse people. There are just a handful standing around..

MANAV
My name is Manav. I'm just one of you. I haven't come to lecture you on corruption, or the system. I have just one question for you: What compelled this man to slap the administration?

MANAV
मेरा नाम मानव है... और मैं आप ही के बीच का हूँ... मैं यहाँ Corruption.. या System पे भाषण देने नहीं आया हूँ... मेरा बस एक ही सवाल है आपसे... क्यूँ ये आदमी... यहाँ के Administration को थप्पड़ मारने पर मजबूर हो गया...

A few people from the gathering shout..

MAN-1
What he did was right!

MAN-1
अच्छा किया!... बहुत अच्छा किया...

MAN-2
Just what was needed!

MAN-2
उसी की ज़रूरत थी!

MAN-3
The Professor was off his head.

MAN-3
Actually, मास्टर जी का खिसक गया था!

Manav picks up on that..

MANAV
Precisely! He lost his head with anger. Just as you are furious. And, fed up.

MANAV
सही कहा आपने... उनके दिमाग़ में आग लगी हुई है!... आप लोगों के दिमाग़ में भी आग़ लगी हुई है... तंग आ चुके हैं लोग...

Suddenly a few Municipal vans with Ladders arrive and the workers begin to tear the freshly put up hoardings down –

S.I., DURGALAL
Remove this poster, now!

S.I., DURGALAL
फाड़ो इस Poster को... हटाओ ये सब...

One of the young men protests –

YOUNG MAN-1
Look at this!

YOUNG MAN-1
ये क्या हो रहा है?...

YOUNG MAN-2
What're you doing?!

YOUNG MAN-2
अरे ऐऽ क्या कर रहे हैं आप लोग...

S.I., DURGALAL
Government orders. Tear this poster... immediately!

S.I., DURGALAL
सरकार का Order है... अरे जल्दी करो... फाड़ के फेंको ये सब...

Manav has been continuing with his speech pointing at the Municipal workers..

MANAV
Do you see this atrocity? They won't even let us speak!

MANAV
आप देख रहे हैं... किस तरह का अत्याचार हो रहा है यहाँ... किस तरह हमें बोलने नहीं दिया जा रहा?!...

However, the municipal workers with the help of a few constables who have joined them for help, begin to clear off the struggling crowd.

And then, Arjun approaches him.

ARJUN
Hey, hey, Mr. Leader! Where the hell have you dropped from?

ARJUN
अरे ऐ नेता जीऽ... कहाँ से आ टपके आप? –

MANAV
From Delhi!

MANAV
दिल्ली से...

ARJUN
Then why are you lecturing here? If you had a problem, you should've come to me. I'm the leader here. I've slogged my butt off for every family here. Be it floods, storms, drought, weddings, funerals – Arjun Singh is always there! Without my permission, no party can even raise a flag in this district. And, you think you can just land here and begin blasting your speeches?!

ARJUN
दिल्ली... तो यहाँ भाषणबाजी काहे कर रहे हैं?... कोई Problem था तो हमें काहे नहीं बताए – हम Leader हैं यहाँ के...सालों से घिस–घिस के सेवा किए हैं Area का – एक–एक Family का ख़याल रखा है... आँधी हो – तूफ़ान हो – बाढ़ हो – सूखाड़ हो – शादी हो – श्राद्ध हो – अर्जुन सिंह हर Time हाज़िर रहता है... बिना हमें बताए कोई Party हमारे District में झंडा तक नहीं उठाता – और आप हैं कि सीधे हवाई जहाज से गाँधी चौक पर Landing करेंगे और लगेंगे भाषण झाड़ने!?...

Manav looks quite zapped at this dressing down. He tries to tell Arjun..

MANAV
See, Mr. Arjun, I am not trying to be a leader here. I just want to get my uncle released.

MANAV
देखिए अर्जुन जी... मैं यहाँ कोई नेतागिरी करने नहीं आया हूँ... बस अपने बाउजी को छुड़ाने की कोशिश कर रहा हूँ –

Arjun points to the poster..

ARJUN *(frowning)*
You mean Dwarka Anand?

ARJUN *(frowning)*
मतलब ये द्वारका आनंद?

MANAV
Yes.

MANAV
जी...

TEA SHOP AT GANDHI CHOWK – INT/EXT – DAY

Arjun and Manav at the Tea shop close to Gandhi Chowk –

ARJUN
That slap was inevitable. The rascal collector is totally corrupt.

ARJUN
थप्पड़ तो पड़ना ही था उस Collector को... Totally भ्रष्ट है साला –

MANAV
But, how do we twist his arm now?

MANAV
पर उस पर Pressure कैसे बनाया जाये...

ARJUN
Amassing crowds is not a problem. But that won't affect the shameless fellow. We need to light a cracker under his pop's chair!

ARJUN
भीड़ तो मैं ऐसे इकट्ठा कर दूँ... मगर सिर्फ़ उससे उसके पेट की खीर खट्टी नहीं होने वाली... बड़ा घाघ है साला... किसी तरह उसके बाप की कुर्सी के नीचे Bomb फोड़ना होगा!...

MANAV
Pop?

MANAV
बाप?...

ARJUN
That bloody minister – Balram Singh.

ARJUN
वो मंत्री साला... बलराम सिंह...

Manav is thinking...

MANAV IN AMBIKAPUR/

YASMIN's CHANNEL's OFFICE- EXT/INT: DAY

Yasmin at her desk. One of the Channel reporters comes in flashing a tape..

REPORTER
Hey Yasmin! Check this out!

REPORTER
Hey Yasmin! इसको देखो ज़रा...

YASMIN
What is this?

YASMIN
क्या है ये?

REPORTER
Real juicy stuff! Last night a Home Minister from a state was with a call-girl. We have some wild footage!

REPORTER
Real Juicy Stuff.. कल रात को एक State के Home Minister दिल्ली आये थे – Call girl तमन्ना के साथ उनकी रंगीन रात का Footage है...

Yasmin frowns..

YASMIN
So?

YASMIN
तो?

REPORTER
It's a sensational story! Let's air it.

REPORTER
मज़ेदार Story है –Channel पे डाल दें इसको!

Yasmin takes the tape. Sounds incredulous.

YASMIN
That's none of our concern... Never! You guys! This is cheap journalism. Completely unethical. What people do in their personal lives, is none of our concern.

YASMIN
Never! तुम लोग भी ना – ये Cheap Journalism है... Completely unethical... हम लोग इतने नीचे Stoop नहीं करते – और कोई अपनी Personal life में क्या करता है... That's none of our concern...

Meanwhile the Channel Boss who has walked in looking at a paper laughs as he addresses Yasmin..

SANDEEP

Yasmin, this is the Prime Minister, for God's sake! How can you ask him such questions?

SANDEEP

यास्मिन, ये Prime Minister हैं... I mean उनसे तुम ऐसे सवाल कैसे पूछ सकती हो –

Yasmin who has gotten busy arranging her things, turns back and says-

YASMIN

Why not? He had said that India believes in growth with social justice, right? But, now that both are clashing, what will he choose?

YASMIN

क्यूँ?... उन्होंने खुद कहा... कि India ऐसे विकास में विश्वास करता है, जहाँ Social Justice भी साथ हो... तो अब जब अक्सर दोनों Clash कर रहे हैं... तो वो कौन सा Choose करेंगे...

Her phone rings. And she smiles as she sees the name 'Manav',

Signaling to Sandeep, who is about to pop another question, she walks away from him to talk.

YASMIN

Hi Manav, what's up?

YASMIN

Hi Manav, what's up?

MANAV

Lots. Listen, I have a fantastic story. A retired school eacher got so fed up with administration, that he slapped the district collector.

MANAV

बहुत कुछ... सुनो, मेरे पास एक Fantastic Story है – एक Retired School Teacher... Administration से इतना तंग आ गया कि Finally उसने जिले के Collector को थप्पड़ मार दिया...

YASMIN

Okay. So, what's the story?

YASMIN

Okay! तो Story क्या है?

MANAV

He is in prison now.

MANAV

अब वो Lockup में बन्द है...

YASMIN

Well, that's hardly surprising.

Pause..

YASMIN

Well, तो इसमें ताज्जुब की क्या बात है?

MANAV *(quietly)*

He is my uncle, Yasmin. My friend Akhilesh's father.

MANAV *(quietly)*

वो मेरे Uncle हैं यास्मिन... मेरे दोस्त अखिलेश के Father...

Yasmin suddenly remembers..

YASMIN

I am so sorry Manav. But... I can't do this story. That would be unprofessional.

YASMIN

I'm so sorry Manav... पर... मैं ये Story नहीं कर पाउँगी... Its not ethical you know...

MANAV

No, it's not like that. His slap has created a storm here. Thousands of people are out on the roads. Just check out the Ambikapur Revolution Site Page on Facebook.

MANAV

नहीं–नहीं वो बात नहीं है... मैं तुम्हें बताना चाहता था कि... उनके थप्पड़ ने कितना बड़ा... तूफ़ान खड़ा कर दिया है... सैकड़ों की तादाद में लोग सड़कों पर आ गये हैं... तुम Facebook पर 'Ambikapur Revolution Site' का Page check करो...

She logs on immediately, as he speaks..

MANAV
You can't imagine how bad the situation is. My uncle's response has triggered off a revolution here!

MANAV
Yasmin, You can't imagine यहाँ हालात कितने ख़राब होते जा रहे हैं... मेरे Uncle के विद्रोह ने एक बहुत बड़ा Revolution खड़ा कर दिया है यहाँ सरकार के ख़िलाफ़...

She sees the Facebook page and various pictures and video content on it. Is surprised. And impressed. Manav continues…

MANAV
A hundred thousand people! All of them demanding his release.

MANAV
करीब एक लाख लोग जमा हो गये हैं... और वो उनकी आज़ादी की Demand कर रहे हैं...

Yasmin interrupts him..

YASMIN *(to Sandeep)*
Sandeep, you'll have to send someone else Japan with the Prime Minister.

YASMIN *(to Sandeep)*
संदीप, तुम्हें किसी और को भेजना पड़ेगा – Prime Minister के साथ... Japan!...

He's incredulous!

SANDEEP
What!?

SANDEEP
What!?

KOTWALI POLICE STATION, AMBIKAPUR– INT/EXT: MORNING

Dwarka sits inside his jail cell, awake and thoughtful while Sumitra sleeps right outside, resting her head on the bench.

Outside, Yasmin walks upto Manav looking a bit baffled – Manav hides his nervousness and manages a faint smile –

MANAV
Thanks for coming...

MANAV
Thanks for coming...

YASMIN
Where's everyone?! You showed me thousands on Facebook.

YASMIN
कहाँ हैं सब!!... तुमने तो Facebook पर हज़ारों लोग दिखाए थे...

Manav looks at Indrojeet Sen who gives a helpless look – Begins to dial a number –

INDROJEET SEN
Can't get through to Arjun.

Manav tries to calm Yasmin –

INDROJEET SEN
अर्जुन का Phone नहीं लग रहा...

MANAV
They must be on their way.

Yasmin is upset – Her Cameraman is unpacking.

MANAV
आते ही होंगे...

JOLLY *(Cameraman)*
What should I shoot, Ma'am?

JOLLY *(Cameraman)*
किसका Shot लूँ Ma'am!

Yasmin ignores him and turns towards Manav.

YASMIN
Listen, Mr. Manav Raghvendra... I didn't leave an important assignment to see your cheap tricks here. And, for God's sake, at least don't treat me like your floozy, Malini Mishra.

YASMIN
Listen Mr. Manav Raghvendra... मैं इतना Important assignment छोड़कर तुम्हारी चालबाज़ी देखने नहीं आई हूँ यहाँ – And for God sake - मुझे अपनी उस Floozy मालिनी मिश्रा के जैसे तो Treat मत करो...

Manav gets serious..

MANAV
I admit that I exaggerated the numbers on Facebook. But, Yasmin, you are needed here. You can't imagine how utterly helpless and disgusted people are with the corruption here. If something is not done now, the public will really revolt. And, that is going to be very violent.

MANAV
माना कि मैंने Face Book पर Number बढ़ा–चढ़ा कर बताये थे... लेकिन, यास्मिन, तुम्हारी बहुत ज़रूरत है यहाँ – तुम सोच भी नहीं सकतीं यहाँ कितना Corruption हो रहा है... लोग एकदम Helpless निराश... यास्मिन, अगर अभी कुछ नहीं किया गया... तो लोग विद्रोह कर देंगे... And that is going to be very Violent...

SADAR POLICE STN. – INT: DAY

As Yasmin is entering the Police Station – one of the Cops stops the Cameraman Jolly.. The Sr.Insp. Durgalal steps forward..

DURGALAL
Sorry, madam. No cameras allowed here.

DURGALAL
Sorry, Madam.. यहाँ Cameras allowed नहीं है अन्दर –

Yasmin shows her Identity Card –

YASMIN
I just want to speak with Mr. Dwarka Anand.

YASMIN
देखिए मैं सिर्फ़ बात करना चाहती हूँ – Mr. Dwarka Anand से...

Dwarka looks up as he hears his name –

DURGALAL
I know who you are, but I can't allow cameras, please.

DURGALAL
मैं आपको जानता हूँ, लेकिन मैं फिर भी Cameras allow नहीं कर सकता – देखिए, Please...

YASMIN *(To her crew)*
Wait outside.

YASMIN *(To her crew)*
बाहर रुकना – मैं आती हूँ..

Yasmin walks up to the Lockup and sits on the low bench close to where Dwarka is seated –

YASMIN
Good Morning Sir..

YASMIN
Good Morning Sir..

Dwarka nods courteously..

As Yasmin looks at this man, calmly sitting on the floor inside the lock-up bunched with some criminals, she wonders –

YASMIN
Why did you slap the D.M.?

YASMIN
आपने D.M. को थप्पड़ क्यूँ मारा?

DWARKA
Because he deserved it.

DWARKA
क्यूँकि वो इसी काबिल थे...

Yasmin looks surprised at the answer –

YASMIN
But, how can you take the law in your own hands?

YASMIN
लेकिन आप कानून को ऐसे अपने हाथ में कैसे ले सकते हैं?...

Dwarka nods..

DWARKA
That's why I'm here! And that is fine.

DWARKA
इसी वजह से तो मैं यहाँ हूँ... And.. that is fine...

YASMIN
Are you aware that there is a massive campaign on outside, for your release? Orchestrated by Manav Raghavendra.

YASMIN
क्या आप जानते हैं कि आपको बाहर निकालने के लिये... एक बहुत बड़ा Campaign चल रहा है?... और उसके पीछे मानव राघवेन्द्र हैं?

Dwarka doesn't answer..

YASMIN *(shakes her head with an indulgent smile)*
And, he tricked me into coming here as well.

YASMIN *(shakes her head with an indulgent smile)*
और उसने अपने Tricks का जाल बुनकर... मुझे भी यहाँ आने पर मजबूर कर दिया...

Arjun arrives with a massive crowd of people. Yasmin comes out, is surprised and runs to start taking visuals of the crowd.

The most common slogan is –
Free Dadu! Free Dadu!

दादू को रिहा करो... *(many times)*

Yasmin asks Arjun...

YASMIN
What are your plans now?

YASMIN
अब क्या Plan है आपका?...

ARJUN
With Manav's brains and our strength, we will finish them!

ARJUN
मानव का Brain और हमारी ताक़त... Band बजा देंगे सालों की...

DIFFERENT PARTS OF THE TOWN – EXT : DAY

A song begins in the background – Binding the spirit of the oppressed – Asking people to come out and face the Sarkaar of Tyrants... Why was common man so brutalised – And now he was not going to take it any more – It is full of humour, scathing, incisive, mocking humour...

They want change and change they will – no matter what the cost!

EXT. GANDHI CHOWK. VARIOUS LOCATIONS: DAY

As the song ends, Yasmin's big story breaks. She stands in the middle of Gandhi Chowk as anchor in front of the camera and begins.

YASMIN

One stone starts a landslide. A spark can light a prairie fire. We're seeing something like that in Ambikapur. On May 25, a highly respected and morally upright Dwarka Anand, a firm believer in Gandhian non-violence, slapped the collector. He was arrested and is in police custody. But, that one slap has created a massive movement here!

YASMIN

हम अक्सर सुनते हैं कि एक पत्थर से Land slide की शुरूआत होती है... एक चिन्गारी पूरे जंगल को राख कर देती है... शायद, यही कुछ हुआ अम्बिकापुर जिले में... 25 मई को यहाँ एक Respected और Morally upright बुजुर्ग... द्वारका आनन्द ने... जो कि गाँधीजी के Non-violent तरीकों में विश्वास करते हैं... एक ज़ोरदार तमाचा यहाँ के Collector के चेहरे पर जड़ दिया... ज़ाहिर है कि उन्हें तुरंत Arrest कर लिया गया और अब वो Lockup में बन्द हैं... लेकिन उस एक तमाचे के कारण... यहाँ एक आन्दोलन खड़ा हो गया है...

In the backdrop are seen teeming crowds chanting slogans for Dwarka's release.

YASMIN

Is this the beginning of a new revolution?

YASMIN

क्या ये एक नये Revolution की शुरूआत है?

Cut to Kalikant Babu watching TV with the CM at the Secretariat.

YASMIN

A revolution that was inevitable. Are the poor and oppressed finally ready to give the rulers an ultimatum? Eradicate corruption, or get out!

YASMIN

एक Revolution जिसका शुरू होना शायद तय था... क्या ग़रीब बेबस लोग Finally सरकार को Ultimatum देने के लिए खड़े हो गये हैं... भ्रष्टाचार हटाओ नहीं तो जाओ...

C.M.'s RESIDENCE OFFICE / CABINET ROOM – EXT/INT : DAY

Over the visuals of the agitation on the T.V...

KALIKANT BABU

Manav Raghavendra is his name. The man behind this upheaval.

KALIKANT BABU

मानव राघवेन्द्र नाम है उसका... वही है इस उपद्रव के पीछे...

C.M.

Yes, but matter is getting serious. We have to do something.

C.M.

हाँ... मगर बात कुछ बढ़ती जा रही है... हमें कुछ करना चाहिए...

KALIKANT BABU

Why! Sir, Ambikapur is Balram Singh's terrain. The DM is his man. If he gets preoccupied with this, he'll be out of our hair.

KALIKANT BABU

क्यूँ!!... Sir देखिए, बलराम सिंह का जिला है अम्बिकापुर... खुद अपनी जात का D.M. का Post करवाया... अब झेलने दीजिए... वहाँ उलझा रहेगा, तो हमारा Headache यहाँ पर कम होगा...

The C.M. nods in agreement. Balram Singh enters the room.

BALRAM SINGH *(To C.M.)*

Namaste.

(To Kalikant)

Namaste Mr. Kalikant.

BALRAM SINGH *(To C.M.)*

नमस्ते...

(To Kalikant)

नमस्ते कालीकांत बाबू...

KALIKANT BABU

Hello.

KALIKANT BABU

नमस्ते...

Balram glances at the TV report that they're watching with an amused eye.

YASMIN
Meanwhile, we conducted polls on Facebook and Twitter. Of 137896 votes, 72% felt the slap was legitimate.

YASMIN
इस बीच हमने SMS के ज़रिए, Facebook पर और Twitter से Voting करवाई... Ambikapur Revolution की Site पर – One Lac Thirty Seven Thousand और Eight Ninety Six लोगों में से बहत्तर प्रतिशत लोगों ने इस थप्पड़ को जायज़ बताया...

Arjun on TV says-

ARJUN
Daduji's hand may have hit the D.M. But, the slap was actually on the government's face!

ARJUN
दादू जी का हाथ भले ही D.M. को लगा हो... लेकिन असली तमाचा... सीधा सरकार के गाल पे पड़ा है!

KALIKANT BABU
Mr. Balram, the media is just exaggerating this. But, you shouldn't worry. You have the CM's full support. And, mine as well.

KALIKANT BABU
बलराम बाबू... ये Media तिल का ताड़ बना रहे हैं – लेकिन आप बिल्कुल मत घबराइये... C.M. सा'ब का Full support है आपको... और हमारा भी...

C.M.
Absolutely! Deal with it firmly. No compromise!

C.M.
बिलकुल!... आप सख़्ती से Deal कीजिए... No compromise!

Balram Singh smile a bitter smile..

BALRAM SINGH
Thank you Sir.. Thank you!
(Turns to go. And, mumbles, audibly.)
With friends like you, who needs enemies.

BALRAM SINGH
Thank you Sir.. Thank you!
(Turns to go. And, mumbles, audibly.)
आपके जैसा Friend हो तो दुश्मन का क्या ज़रूरत है...

BALRAM SINGH's RESIDENCE/OFFICE &

D.M.'s OFFICE – EXT/INT:

Sangram Singh, The D.M. and the S.P. are all on a video conference with Balram Singh.

BALRAM SINGH
You are an idiot, Sangram Singh! I gave you a 5 billion company, but your brains aren't worth a cent. You can't handle even one district?

BALRAM SINGH
भूतिया हैं का आप संग्राम सिंह... अँयँ!... पाँच सौ करोड़ रुपये का Company दिये हैं चलाने को... पाँच पैसा का अकल नहीं है... एक जिला नहीं Handle कर सकते तुम?...

He then addresses the D.M. ..

BALRAM SINGH
And you, Mr. D.M. Why have you created so much tension? In my own district!

BALRAM SINGH
और का D.M. साहब?... काहे एतना Tension पैदा कर दिए हैं?... हमरे ही जिला में बवाल खड़ा करवा दिया –

The Collector looks flushed – He stammers...

D.M.
No, sir.. actually..

D.M.
नहीं Sir वो... Actually वो हम...

BALRAM SINGH
Didn't your father ever slap you in childhood? Imagine this oldie to be your pop. Forgive and forget, pal.

BALRAM SINGH
अरे बचपन में आपके Father आपको थपड़ियाये थे कि नहीं... इ बुढ़ऊ को भी अपना Father समझिए... और Forget and Forgive कीजिए भाई...

Balram Singh turns to the SP..

BALRAM SINGH
And you, Mr. Superintendent? What on earth are you upto?

BALRAM SINGH
क्या S.P. साहेब... क्या गुल खिलाया आपने?...

S.P.
But sir, tensions have really escalated. They have surrounded the police station. I am imposing a curfew.

S.P.
मगर Sir, Tension बहुत बढ़ गया है – कोतवाली घेर लिये हैं सब... हम 144 लगा रहे हैं Town में –

Balram Singh strikes his own forehead –

BALRAM SINGH
Why don't you impose a curfew on my political career as well? Your power has got you drunk!

BALRAM SINGH
अरे हमारे राजनीतिक Career पर ही एक सौ चवालिस काहे नहीं लगा देते हैं आप!!... Power के नशा में एकदम चूर हो गये हैं आप...

POLICE STATION – EXT : MORNING

Next morning as Yasmin arrives, a much stronger crowd of people have arrived.

Suddenly, they are all alarmed with approaching blaring of sirens... A cavalcade of cars arrive. The cops push the crowd making way for the vehicles –

Home Minister Balram Singh gets off and Arjun begins the slogan of 'Murdabad.. 'Down with Balram Singh'... A few hundreds of the Minister's party workers too have arrived with the cavalcade and soon begin to shout pro Balram Singh slogans...

Balram Singh turns around and signals his men to stop shouting slogans...

CROWD
Release, Dadu!
Down with Balram Singh!

CROWD
दादू को रिहा करो... *(many times)*
बलराम सिंह... मुर्दाबाद... *(many times)*

BALRAM'S PEOPLE
Long live Balram Singh..

BALRAM'S PEOPLE
बलराम सिंह... जिंदाबाद... *(many times)*

ARJUN
Down with Balram Singh!

ARJUN
बलराम सिंह... मुर्दाबाद... बलराम सिंह... मुर्दाबाद...

CROWD
बलराम सिंह...

CROWD
बलराम सिंह...

ARJUN
Down with Balram Singh!

ARJUN
मुर्दाबाद...

LAATON KE BHOOT...

While shooting the rally scenes, the junior artistes suddenly refused to work. When asked the reason, they revealed that they did not want to hit Mr. Bachchan! Even with fake lathis. Finally it took a few good hearted jokes from Big B himself to get them to pick up the lathis!

बहुत हो चुका अब न सहेंगे
अपना हक हम लेकर रहेंगे।

Balram stops his own sloganeering...

BALRAM SINGH
Stop this sloganeering. Stop it!

BALRAM SINGH
बन्द कीजिए... बन्द कीजिए नारेबाज़ी... बंद कीजिए...

He then turns to Arjun's men- Smiles-

BALRAM SINGH
You people, please continue. The public has a right to be angry. Let them shout. Please continue. And himself begins to lead-

BALRAM SINGH
चलिए चालू रखिए आप लोग... अरे Public का गुस्सा है... अँयँ... उसको Chance दीजिए... Chance दीजिए उसको... हाँ–हाँ चालू रखिए आप लोग... चालू रखिए...

BALRAM SINGH
Down with Balram Singh!

BALRAM SINGH
बलराम सिंह – मुर्दाबाद...

The people look confused. Balram turns to his own people and exhorts them -

BALRAM SINGH
Down with Balram Singh!

BALRAM SINGH
बलराम सिंह – मुर्दाबाद...

BULBUL SINGH
Down with Balram Singh! Down with Balram Singh! Down..

BULBUL SINGH
बलराम सिंह – मुर्दाबाद... बलराम सिंह – मुर्दाबाद... बलराम्...

BALRAM SINGH *(To Bulbul Singh)*
Idiot!

BALRAM SINGH *(To Bulbul Singh)*
गधा कहीं का...

No one speaks..

BALRAM SINGH
The public has a right to be upset. The mistake is mine. Getting busy with state matters, I neglected my own home. And, an injustice occurred. I admit my mistake. And, I will rectify it today, right now!

BALRAM SINGH
Public total right है... इनको हक़ है हमको Down करने का – काहे से कि हमसे Mistake हुआ है... हम State के Problem में थोड़ा Busy हो गये थे... और अपना ही घर अनदेखा हो गया – जहाँ एक भारी अन्याय हो गया... अरे मान लिए कि Mistake हो गया है – अऽ हम इसको Correct करेंगे... आज... अऽ अभी!!...

Balram Singh walks into the Police station and a little later, as everyone waits, appears followed by Dwarka, Sumitra and a dozen other officers.

The crowd is still confused as Balram Singh leads Dwarka and Sumitra to the stage..

BALRAM SINGH
Come, come, sir.. please come.
(to band guyson the stage)
You band guys, clear off now.
(on the mike)
I consider Mr. Dwarka as the guardian of Ambikapur. So, there is no shame in accepting a punishment from him. Hence, our

BALRAM SINGH
आइये... आइये... आइये – आइये... आइये... हट जाइये... आइये...
(to band guyson the stage)
चलिए चलिए... Band बाजा लोग... चलिए... चलिए हो गया...
(on the mike)
द्वारका बाबू को... हमलोग... अम्बिकापुर का Guardian मानते हैं... तो Guardian से Punishment लेने में कोई शर्म नहीं होना चाहिए... अऽ इसी

collector has withdrawn his complaint and apologises to Daduji. And, I hereby announce his freedom!

बात को मानते हुए हमारे Collector साहेब ने... अपना Complaint Return लेने का फ़ैसला किया है... औ दादू जी से माफ़ी माँगते हुए... हम उनकी आज़ादी का Announcement करते हैं...

The crowd erupts – In cheers and claps –

ARJUN
Long live Daduji!

ARJUN
दादू जी... जिन्दाबाद... दादू जी... जिन्दाबाद...

PUBLIC
Long live Daduji!

PUBLIC
दादू जी... जिन्दाबाद... दादू जी... जिन्दाबाद...

While Manav continues to stand a little away close to Yasmin, Arjun jumps on the stage and touching Dwarka's feet he says..

ARJUN
You cannot expel me from school today, sir.

ARJUN
दादू जी आज आप हमें School से नहीं निकाल सकते...

Dwarka embraces him.. He looks quite calm and composed.

Meanwhile Balram Singh has signaled to the D.M. who has got a big replica of a cheque on the stage..

BALRAM SINGH
On this happy occasion
(to his man asks for Cheque)
I request Daduji to kindly accept this gift from the government.

BALRAM SINGH
अब इस... Happy Time में... दादू जी से Hearty निवेदन है...
(to his man asks for Cheque)
लाइये... कि एक... एक छोटा सा भेंट स्वीकार करें...

Seeing the cheque – in Balram's hand people roar and dance..

Surprisingly Dwarka makes no move to collect the cheque from the Minister.

Dwarka walks up and takes the microphone.

DWARKA
When I was behind bars, I often thought of my son Akhilesh. And wondered what he would've done, if he were alive. And, I realized that probably he would've done what got done here. Perhaps Akhilesh's absence is being filled now. Perhaps I have found another son.

DWARKA
मैं जब यहाँ... सलाखों के अन्दर था... तो अक्सर मुझे अपने बेटे अखिलेश की याद आई... तो बस यही सोचता था कि उसके रहते यदि मैं अन्दर गया होता... तो वो क्या करता... तो मुझे ये एहसास हुआ कि शायद वो भी वही करता जो... अब हुआ... अब लग रहा है कि... अखिलेश की कमी पूरी हो गई है... शायद... मुझे एक और बेटा मिल गया...

Dwarka directly looks at Manav. The crowd turns to look at him –

Dwarka gestures to him to come to the stage.. Manav is too shocked and confused to move.. Arjun raises the slogan..

ARJUN
Long live Manav! Long live Manav!
People roar –
Long live Manav! Long live Manav!

ARJUN
मानव भइया – जिन्दाबाद... मानव भइया – जिन्दाबाद...
People roar –
मानव भाई... जिन्दाबाद... *(many times)*

Arjun and his men move towards Manav and lift him to transport him through the crowd onto the stage..

On the stage Dwarka hugs Manav.

BALRAM SINGH
Splendid, splendid!
(laughs)
This is double happiness! So Mr. Dwarka, kindly accept this cheque now.

BALRAM SINGH
वाह भाइयों!... वाह... वाह–वाह...
(laughs)
ये तो Double Happy Time हो गया... तो द्वारका बाबू... उसे कृपा करके ग्रहण किया जाये...

He extends the cheque. Dwarka looks at him but instead of taking the cheque he says -

DWARKA
Pardon me, but I cannot accept this cheque.

DWARKA
माफ़ कीजिएगा मंत्री जी – मगर मैं ये Cheque ले नहीं सकता...

Balram looks insulted – The crowd too is surprised..

BALRAM SINGH
But why?

BALRAM SINGH
अऽ... But- Why, क्यों?...

DWARKA
I didn't slap the DM only because my cheque was getting delayed. It was also for those millions of common people who have to wait for years on end just to receive their legitimate claims.

DWARKA
उस दिन जब हमने D.M. साहब पर हाथ उठाया था... तो वो बस... इसलिए नहीं कि हमें इस Cheque को मिलने में देरी हो रही थी... ये उन हज़ारों–लाखों लोगों के... सालों–साल तक... कलक्टरी के दफ़्तरों में... जायज़ Claims को पाने की देरी के लिए भी था...

BALRAM SINGH
But, how are the two things connected?

BALRAM SINGH
लेकिन... उसका इससे क्या Connection है?...

DWARKA
They are, Mr. Minister. The frustration, desperation and humiliation that I suffered, is inflicted by your corrupt system on these people every day. So, now all of us will confront your corruption and injustice unitedly. I have a right to this cheque, but I won't accept it until all the pending applications gathering dust in Ambikapur's government offices are cleared.

DWARKA
Connection है मंत्री जी... Connection तो है... जिस आक्रोश... मजबूरी और... शर्मिंदगी को मैंने महसूस किया... वो आपका ये भ्रष्ट System.. उन लाखों लोगों को रोज़... इसी तरह... बेइज्ज़त करता रहता है... तो अब आपके इस Corruption और अन्याय का सामना... हम... सब मिलके करेंगे... ये जो... आपके हाथ में Cheque है... इस पर मेरा अधिकार है... लेकिन मैं इसे तब तक नहीं लूँगा... जब तक आप इस अम्बिकापुर के... सारे सरकारी दफ़्तरों में... सालों से धूल फाँकते एक–एक Application... मुआवज़े... Petitions... और हर तरह के Claims को... Clear नहीं कर देते...

Balram is stunned.

BALRAM SINGH
Tell me, Mr. Dwarka, how many dues and claims are pending in this district?

BALRAM SINGH
अच्छा द्वारका बाबू... हमें ये बताइये कि... कितने Dues और Claims pending हैं इस जिला में?

DWARKA
Do you know that, Mr. Minister? If not, start finding out. Because I'm giving you 30 days for this. And your time starts... now!

DWARKA
क्या आपको मालूम है मंत्री जी?... और अगर नहीं है... तो शुरू कीजिए पता लगाना... क्योंकि मैं आपको... 30 दिनों का वक़्त दे रहा हूँ... और आपका वक़्त शुरू होता है... अब!

Balram begins to almost laugh..

BALRAM SINGH
Is this a joke, Mr. Dwarka?

BALRAM SINGH
द्वारका बाबू... कहीं आप मज़ाक तो नहीं कर रहे हैं –

DWARKA
30 days, Mr Minister! Else the public will really make a joke out of you. Lets go.

DWARKA
तीस दिन, मंत्री जी... 30 days... वर्ना ये जनता सचमुच में आपके साथ मज़ाक कर बैठेगी... चलो बेटा...

Slogans...

ARJUN
दादू जी...

ARJUN
दादू जी...

CROWD
Long live Daduji!

CROWD
जिंदाबाद...

So saying, he takes Manav and gets off the stage. As they get off the stage, almost everyone in the audience begins to walk behind Dwarka, Manav, Arjun and Sumitra.. The Minister is left standing on the stage with the cheque replica.

Yasmin catches up with the bitter looking Balram Singh on the stage..

YASMIN
He refused your compensation. What would you like to say about that?

YASMIN
उन्होंने आपका Compensation स्वीकार नहीं किया – आप क्या कहना चाहेंगे इसके बारे में...

Balram throws the cheque on the stage and marches off.. The officers and his men follow him – Yasmin picks up the cheque and with her back to the receding crows, she reports..

YASMIN
This cheque of 2.5 million is going to re-write Ambikapur's history. Acquitted of the charge of slapping the DM, Mr. Dwarka Anand has thrown an open challenge to both the government and the administration. 30 days to clear the countless files buried under corruption! Interesting times ahead. But today, a 70-year old school teacher has given a powerful push to the jammed wheels of democracy. With cameraman Jolly Pinto - Yasmin Ahmed, Ambikapur.

YASMIN
पच्चीस लाख का ये Cheque... आज अम्बिकापुर में शायद एक नया इतिहास लिखेगा... District Collector को थप्पड़ मारने के आरोप से रिहा हुए द्वारका आनन्द ने... सरकार और Administration दोनों को खुली चुनौती दी है... तीस दिनों का वक़्त है... और Corruption के बोझ तले दबी हुई लाखों फाइलें... क्या होगा ये तो समय ही बताएगा... लेकिन आज एक सत्तर साल के एक School Teacher ने लोकतंत्र के Jam हुए चक्के को एक ज़ोरदार धक्का ज़रूर दिया है... गाँधी चौक, अम्बिकापुर से... Cameraman Jolly Pinto के साथ – मैं यास्मिन अहमद, ABP News...

Dwarka walks through the streets at Gandhi Chowk.. Transformer Baba jumps in the middle of the crowd - jumping and dancing with joy..

TRANSFORMER BABA
Kabir stands in the market place. Holding aloft a burning torch!
Whosoever sets his house on fire. Is welcome to join him!!

TRANSFORMER BABA
कबिरा खड़ा बजार में, लिये लुकाटी हाथ।
जो घर फूँके आपना, चले हमारे साथ।।

As Dwarka reaches his compound – it seems like the whole town has walked with him.. Baskets full of laddoos are being distributed and firecrackers lit.

At the gate he tells Manav..

DWARKA
Come son..

DWARKA
आओ बेटा...

Manav looks overwhelmed – Sumitra leads him inside.. Dwarka looks at the multitude who have gathered and thanks them for their support..

DWARKA COLONY – INT/EXT: DAY

DOWN STAIRS LIVING ROOM

The living room and the verandah is teeming with Manav, Yasmin, Arjun, Indrojeet Sen, neighbours, youngsters and town's people –

YASMIN
Daduji, do you think that the government will take any action on your ultimatum?

YASMIN
दादूजी, आपको क्या लगता है... सरकार आपके इस Ultimatum पर कोई Action लेगी?...

Sumitra hands over tea to Dwarka and remarks -

SUMITRA
This Government is not going to do anything!

SUMITRA
ये सरकार कुछ नहीं करने वाली –

Dwarka smiles –

DWARKA
Sumitra is right. We'll have to do everything. We need to first find out about all the pending cases.

DWARKA
ठीक बोलती है सुमित्रा... हमें ही सब कुछ करना होगा... हमें किसी तरह... जितने Pending cases हैं उनकी जानकारी जमा करनी होगी –

ARJUN
But how, Daduji? So many villages, towns... must be millions of cases.

ARJUN
पता कैसे लगायेंगे दादूजी... इतने गाँव... ताल्लुके... लाखों Cases होंगे...

MANAV
If we go to them, it'll cost us time. Instead, they could reach us easily, in less time.

MANAV
बजाय हम पहुँचें उनके पास – जिसमें बहुत सारा वक़्त लग सकता है... वो हमारे पास बड़ी आसानी से और कम वक़्त में पहुँच सकते हैं –

DWARKA
But... how?

DWARKA
पर... कैसे?...

Manav nods.. Looks at a couple of youngsters..

MANAV
Get me a whiteboard.

MAN
Sure, bhaiya..

As they run to find one...

MANAV
How many blocks are there in Ambikapur?

ARJUN
Seven.

MANAV
And how many councils in each block?

SUMITRA
About 30-35.

The kids have placed the easel and the white board.. Manav writes –

MANAV
7 times 35.. 245. We have to reach 245 councils. We use a three-pronged strategy. Mark the entry-exit points of the blocks. Then, train volunteers in each council area.
(calculates on the board 245 x 2 = 490)
Can we get 490 educated people, Arjun?

ARJUN
I can get you double that number. In 24 hours.

MANAV
Good! We train them to photocopy, scan, email and store. Open collection centres in the marketplace of every council. Two: We publicise Daduji's appeal through pamphlets, cable TV. Play his audio-visual recordings on social media day & night. Cycles, rickshaws and horse-carts will announce the locations of collection centers. Yasmin, if you can get some news channels to cover the appeal story, that would be the icing on the cake. Arjun, gather volunteers. Sumitra, conduct the training. And Indrojeet, take charge of the documentation. This way we can gather 70-80% the claims.

MANAV
White Board ले आओ...

MAN
जी, भइया...

MANAV
अर्जुन, अम्बिकापुर में कितने Blocks होंगे?

ARJUN
सात...

MANAV
और हर Block में कितने पंचायत होंगे?

SUMITRA
कुछ तीस पैंतीस...

MANAV
सात... और पैंतीस... 245.. तो हमें 245 पंचायत तक पहुँचना है... हम Three pronged strategy कर सकते हैं... पहले Blocks के Entry Exit point पर... और फिर पंचायत में Volunteers को train करके...
(calculates on the board 245 x 2 = 490)
इतने पढ़े–लिखे लोग मिल जायेंगे यहाँ?

ARJUN
इससे तो दो गुना ज़्यादा इकट्ठा कर देंगे – चौबीस घंटे में...

MANAV
Good!.. इनकी Xeroxing, Scanning, E-mailing और Storing की Training के साथ–साथ... हर पंचायत के बाज़ार और नुक्कड़ पर... Collection Centre लगाएँ... Two... अख़बार – Pamphlets, Local cable TV – Social media और... बाउजी की appeal record करके... Audio-Video दोनों दिन–रात चलायें... Cycle, Rickshaw, टाँगा सभी पर घूम–घूम कर... हर गाँव टोले में Announcement करके... Collection Centre की Location बताएँ... यास्मिन, अगर दो–तीन Local Channel से बात करके अगर... दो–तीन Stories Appeal करवा दें तो सोने पे सुहागा... अर्जुन Volunteers जमा कर लें... सुमित्रा Training programme की देखभाल कर लें... और इन्द्रजीत आप... कागज़ी काम... Forms और Logistics देख लें... इससे 70 से 80 percent claims की Copies तो... जमा की ही जा सकती हैं...

Everyone has been listening to him in silence – their attention growing into admiration.. Arjun steps forward and hugs him..

ARJUN
Wow boss! All we needed was you. With you in the team, we'll be unstoppable.

ARJUN
वाह् Boss, बस तुम्हारी ही ज़रूरत थी हमको... अब तुम हमारे साथ हो तो कोई नहीं रोक सकता...

SUMITRA
Absolutely!

SUMITRA
बिल्कुल भैया...

Dwarka brings them all to reality..

DWARKA
Hold on. Manav has a flight to catch tomorrow. He has a business to take care of. And, his own life to live.

DWARKA
अऽ... वो सब तो ठीक है, लेकिन... मानव की Flight है कल सुबह... यहीं अटका रहा तो इतना बड़ा उसका जो कारोबार है वो चलेगा कैसे... आख़िर उसकी भी तो ज़िन्दगी है...

It is an awkward moment for all of them..

DWARKA HOUSE- EXT/INT: AFTERNOON

INT: UPSTAIRS...

Manav is on the terrace, talking to his Secretary Nancy, on the phone..

MANAV
Yes, I'm taking the first flight back tomorrow. No, no..

MANAV
हाँ, मैं सुबह की Flight से ही वापस आ रहा हूँ... नहीं–नहीं...

Yasmin comes down the stairs with her Laptop...

YASMIN
Sumi, may I use your computer? Mine's crashed. Need to file a report.

YASMIN
सुमी, मैं तुम्हारा Computer use कर लूँ... मेरा Hang हो गया है... एक Report file करनी है...

SUMITRA
Sure. But mine is too slow. Why don't you use Akhilesh's computer?

SUMITRA
हाँ ज़रूर... पर मेरा बहोत Slow है... अखिलेश का Comp क्यूँ नहीं Use करती...

She comes up with her and turns the computer on..

SUMITRA
Am booting it for the first time in months. Since..

SUMITRA
इतने महीनों में पहली बार On कर रही हूँ... जबसे...

Yasmin realises the heaviness in Sumitra's voice and comforts her..

Dwarka calls from downstairs –

DWARKA
Sumitra!

DWARKA
अरे सुमित्रा...

SUMITRA
Coming, Dad.

SUMITRA
आई बाबूजी...

Yasmin notices Manav on the terrace busy on his phone..

MANAV
Fix my meetings for tomorrow. I'll take the night flight to Paris. The contract should've been signed 10 days ago. Ask Andre to ready the papers. I'll head straight to HQ. And yes, tell Hari to..

MANAV
मेरी सारे Meetings कल के लिए Fix करो... रात की Flight लूँगा Paris के लिए... Contract 10 दिन पहले ही Sign होना था... तुम Andre से कहना कि Papers ready करे... Airport से सीधा Headquarters जाउँगा... और सुनो... हरि को बोलना –

Just as she begins to press the keys Akhilesh's computer comes alive and a file opens up.. She is surprised... She calls out..

YASMIN
Manav!

YASMIN
मानव...

MANAV
Ask Khatri to fix my meeting with the Minister.

MANAV
वो खत्री से बात करे... मंत्री से Meeting Fix करे... Ok..

Manav comes in – She is still reading the letter..

MANAV
Yes?

MANAV
हुँ...

YASMIN
Manav, had Akhilesh submitted his resignation?

YASMIN
मानव, अखिलेश ने Resignation Letter दिया था क्या?

MANAV
No,
(as he reads)
he never told me.

MANAV
नहीं तो...
(as he reads)
मुझे तो बताया नहीं...

YASMIN
He refers to some confidential report.

YASMIN
किसी Confidential Report की बात लिखी हुई है...

MANAV
This resignation raises several questions.

MANAV
कई सवाल खड़े कर रहा है ये Resignation Letter...

N.H. OFFICE-EXT/INT: EVENING

Manav and Yasmin with the Superintendent –

SUPERINTENDENT
No way. Resignation is out of question. On the contrary, the minister had praised his work and made him in-charge of all the projects of the district. Manav looks at Yasmin..

SUPERINTENDENT
नहीं नहीं... Resignation का तो सवाल ही पैदा नहीं होता... बल्कि उलटे मंत्री जी ने उनके काम की तारीफ़ की थी – पूरे District के Project का Incharge बनाया था...

YASMIN
What about the flyover mishap's enquiry report?

YASMIN
Flyover हादसे की Enquiry Report...

SUPERINTENDENT
The minister ordered that himself. From an international firm, Engineers Audit. The report is on our website. It was a human error.

SUPERINTENDENT
वो तो मंत्री जी ने खुद Order किया था – International firm है... Engineers Audit Ltd. .. हमारी Website पे पूरी Report available है... It was a human error...

As Manav and Yasmin come out – Ramlal the peon points out to the spot..

RAMLAL
This is where Mr. Akhilesh sat. Always busy. Always cared for the poor.

RAMLAL
यहीं तो बैठते थे अखिलेश बाबू – दिन–रात Busy.. ग़रीब का बहुत ख़याल था उनको –

While Yasmin stands rooted Manav has walked upto the corner – Manav gets emotional as he notices the Screensaver.. It's the same one from the FUTURE IV clip.. The man whose work station it now is, comes up behind Manav..

THE MAN
I really liked the Screensaver. So I didn't change it.

THE MAN
I really liked the Screensaver... तो मैंने Change नहीं किया...

Manav smiles at him..

DWARKA HOUSE – EXT/INT: NIGHT

Dwarka has been waiting for Manav... As Yasmin and he enter the gate he gets up from his chair in the verandah.. Yasmin whispers to Manav..

YASMIN
You want to tell uncle?

YASMIN
Uncle को बताना है?

MANAV
No, not now.

MANAV
नहीं अभी नहीं...

Yasmin nods.. Manav addresses Dwarka..

MANAV
You're still up, Dad?

MANAV
बाउजी आप सोये नहीं अब तक...

Dwarka leads him into the house..

DWARKA
I thought since you're leaving tomorrow.. I couldn't even speak with you properly.

DWARKA
बस बेटा... सोचा... कल निकल जाओगे तुम सुबह... ठीक से तुमसे बात नहीं कर पाये...

He puts his arm around Manav and walks into his room while Sumitra meets up with Yasmin –

SUMITRA
Should I serve the food?

SUMITRA
मैं खाना लगवा दूँ...

INSIDE Dwarka's room..

Dwarka eases onto his bed resting on his pillow.. Manav covers Dwarka's feet with the blanket..

Dwarka holds Manav's hands for a long moment..

A lump has begun to form in Manav's throat..

MANAV
Dad, you should rest now.

MANAV
बाउजी... अब आप... आराम कीजिए...

DWARKA
Sit, son. I just wanted to say that... I completely misunderstood you. So many times, I.. used such harsh words...

DWARKA
बैठो... बस बेटा यही... कहना चाहता था तुमसे कि... तुम्हें मैं ठीक से समझ नहीं पाया... कई बार... बड़ी ही... कर्कश बातें कह दीं तुम्हें...

MANAV
Dad, what are you saying!

MANAV
बाबूजी... ये आप कैसी बातें कर रहे हैं...

DWARKA
Now I understand why Akhilesh loved you so much. After his death, I was stunned. So many times I wondered, if I would be able to pull through.

DWARKA
अब पता चला कि अखिलेश... तुमसे इतना स्नेह क्यूँ करता था... उसके जाने के बाद... जैसे... सून्न पड़ गया था मैं... कई बार ऐसा लगा कि... पता नहीं पार लगा पाउँगा या नहीं...

Manav looks at Dwarka..

DWARKA *[contd.]*
But, now that I have you.. that void is filling up. Thank you, son.. thank you.

DWARKA *[contd.]*
लेकिन... अब तुम आ गये हो तो... उसकी कमी... दूर हो गयी है.... Thank you बेटा... Thank you...

Manav is choking as he notices drops of tears slipping out of Dwarka's eyes..

MANAV
Dad, you're everything now, for me too.

MANAV
बाउजी... मेरे लिए भी तो अब... सब कुछ आप ही हो...

DWARKA
Son, you will leave tomorrow. Your business...

DWARKA
बेटा कल तुम... चले जाओगे... तुम्हारा सब –

MANAV
I'm not going anywhere, Dad. Until this 30-day mission of yours is done, I'll be right here. With you.

MANAV
मैं कहीं नहीं जा रहा बाउजी... जब तक आपका ये... 30 दिन का Mission पूरा नहीं हो जाता... मैं यहीं रहूँगा... आपके साथ...

Dwarka is looking at him.. His face relaxing into an enlightened fulfillment.. Manav covers him with the blanket – And helps him lie down..

MANAV
You should rest now. We have to begin the campaign tomorrow.

MANAV
अब आप आराम कीजिए... कल सुबह अभियान शुरू करना है...

There is a smile on Dwarka's face as he shuts his eyes..

VARIOUS LOCATIONS:

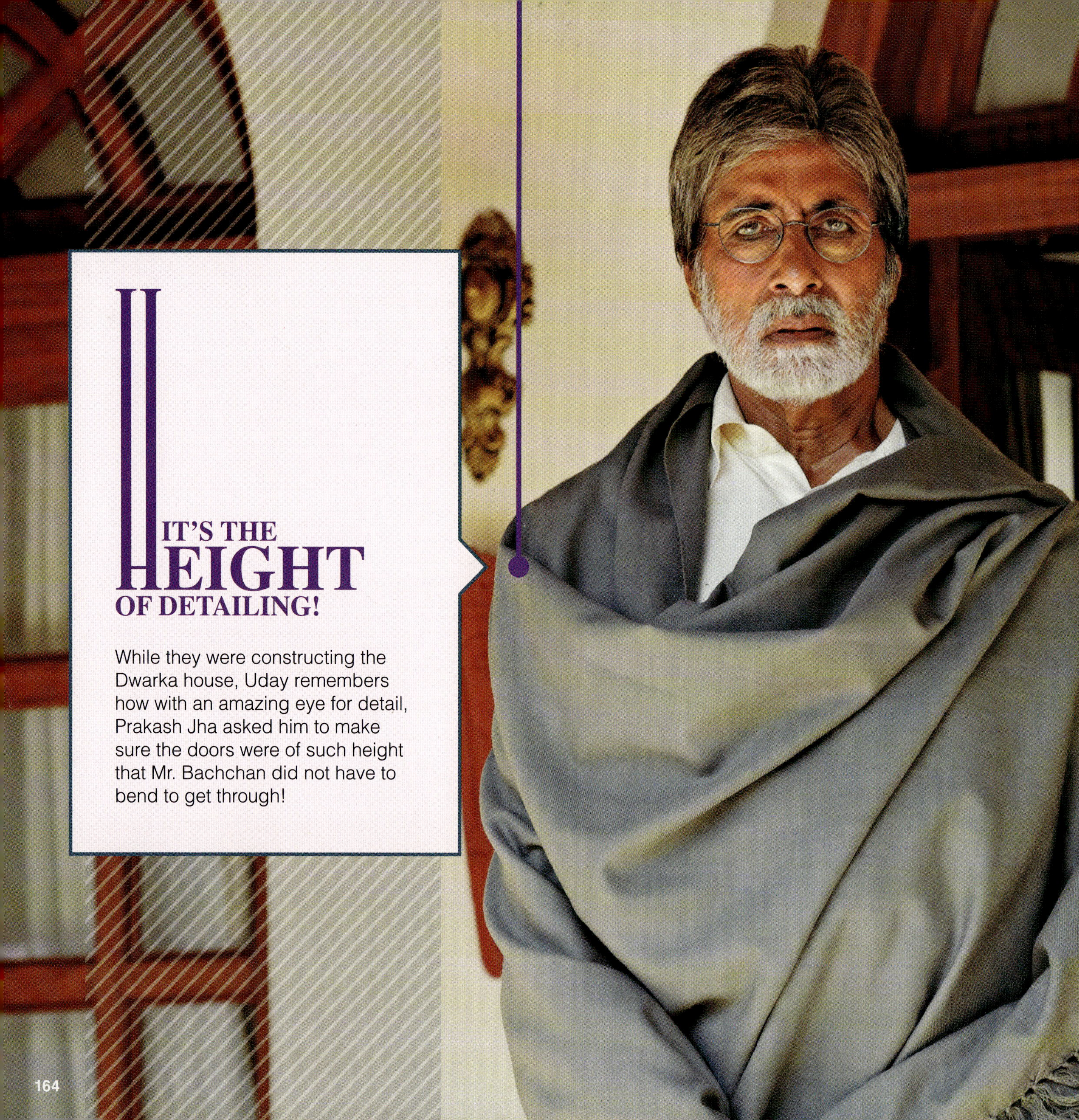

IT'S THE HEIGHT OF DETAILING!

While they were constructing the Dwarka house, Uday remembers how with an amazing eye for detail, Prakash Jha asked him to make sure the doors were of such height that Mr. Bachchan did not have to bend to get through!

OVER THE TRACK OF JANTA ROCKS...

Montage of applications being collected.. Young people creating Facebook pages on the campaign.. Manav distributing a dozen tablets to a bunch of village kids and teaching them how to use it.. Indrojeet Sen and his bunch of lawyers typing out R.T.I. applications and filing them in government offices..Youngsters from villages carrying bundles of documents on their motorbikes..In far away villages applications being scanned, photocopied.. On the internet and social media site they update the status on the campaign..

SECRETARIAT – CABINET MEETING HALL: DAY

The Government has called an all Party meeting to discuss the grave situation.. Gauri Shankar's expression shows his tough, challenging stance!

GAURI SHANKAR
If a special session is not summoned to implement the public demand, our party workers will take to the streets and start a massive movement.

GAURI SHANKAR
अगर जनता की माँगों को पूरा करने के लिए... विधान–सभा का Special session नहीं बुलाया गया... तो हमारी Party सड़कों पर उतर के भीषण आंदोलन करेगी देख लीजिए आप लोग...

BALRAM SINGH *(very forcefully)*
If any legislator takes to the streets, he will lose the voters' confidence. You're attacking the very branch on which you are perched, Mr. Gaurishankar.
(Pause. They know this is the truth.)
Every legislator of every party puts in a lot of hard work, patience and investment to win an election. Only so he can earn something for 5 years. No one has the right to jeopardize his investment! If we let a handful of people blackmail democratically elected leaders, this fire will get out of control. And, you can then kiss your legislative career goodbye.

BALRAM SINGH *(very forcefully)*
कोई भी विधायक अगर सड़कों पर उतरेगा... तो Voters का विश्वास खो बैठेगा... जिस डाल पे बैठे हो उसी डाल को काट रहे हो आप, गौरी शंकर बाबू!... अँयँ...
(Pause. They know this is the truth.)
छोटा–बड़ा हर Party का विधायक बहुत मेहनत...तिकड़म और Investment करके चुनाव जीतता है – कि बेचारा पाँच साल कुछ कमाएगा... और किसी को हक़ नहीं बनता है कि उसके Investment को ख़तरे में डाले... अरे अगर हमने मुट्ठी भर लोगों को लोकतंत्र से चुने गये Leaders को Blackmail करने दिया... तो ये आग Out of Control हो जायेगा... फिर Goodbye कीजिए अपने Legislative career को...

GAURISHANKAR RESIDENCE- INT: DAY

Gaurishankar proposes to Indrojeet..

GAURISHANKAR
Your tactics are clever. Demands are bang-on too. But even you know that without political support, it'll amount to zero. The common man is not free to come and shout slogans every day. For that, you need solid workers from the BMD Party. Invite us to your platform. We'll shake the government up!

GAURISHANKAR
चाल अच्छी है आप लोगों की... Demand भी सही है... मगर इतना तो आप लोग भी जानते हैं – कि बिना Political support के Everything becomes zero... अरे आम आदमी थोड़ी बैठेगा रोज नारा लगाने के लिए... उसके लिए आपको चाहिए B.M.D. Party का Solid worker... हमें Invite कीजिए अपना Platform पर... हिला के रख देंगे इस सरकार को...

VARIOUS LOCATIONS- EXT/INT: DAY

Manav reacts to the proposal...

MANAV
BMD is a communal party, Indrojeet. We will have nothing to do with them.

MANAV
भारतीय मुक्ति दल Communal Party है, इन्द्रजीत... हमारा इनसे कोई मेल नहीं हो सकता...

SONG continues...

COACHING CLASSROOM – INT: DAY

The teacher is teaching about 12 young men..

TEACHER
So that 2c b Cos A...

TEACHER
So that 2c b Cos A...

Shashinath, a young student looks at his watch, gestures with his head to four friends.. they all look restless..

SHASHINATH
Its time. Come, lets go!

SHASHINATH
Time हो गया... चल न यार, चलते हैं...

Just then the teacher turns around..

TEACHER
What is it?

TEACHER
क्या बात है!

SHASHINATH
Sir, we want to go for the campaign that Manav has begun for Daduji's ultimatum.

SHASHINATH
Sir, वो... दादूजी के Ultimatum पर मानव भैया ने जो अभियान चलाया है... हम लोग वहाँ जाना चाहते थे...

The teacher looks at him for a moment..

TEACHER
Now?! You want to leave the class?

TEACHER
अभी!... इस वक़्त... Class छोड़ कर...

Ritesh, one of the boys speaks up..

RITESH
That's what I'm trying to tell him, sir. His dad took a loan to pay his fees here.

RITESH
वही समझा रहा हूँ Sir इसको... Loan लेकर इसके बाबूजी ने यहाँ की फीस जमा की है ...

VIMAL
Sir, none of us want to leave your class. But, he's doing all this for our good.

VIMAL
Sir, आपकी Class छोड़कर कोई नहीं जाना चाहता... मगर वो जो कर रहे हैं... हमारी भलाई के लिए कर रहे हैं...

TEACHER
You good lies in your future, not in politics.

TEACHER
देखो तुम्हारी भलाई सिर्फ़ अपना भविष्य बनाने में है... न कि Politics में...

SHASHINATH
Sir, Manav's not into politics. He speaks of improving the system.

SHASHINATH
Sir, वो Politics नहीं कर रहे हैं... वो तो सरकार के System को दुरुस्त करने की बात कर रहे हैं...

KAILASH
No matter how hard we study, and which degree we get. If the system doesn't improve, what future do we have?

KAILASH
और हम चाहे लाख पढ़ लें – Degree ले लें... जब तक वो Improve नहीं होगा... हमारा भविष्य क्या है...

NAGENDRA
Please sir, we'll take extra classes. But allow us to go.

NAGENDRA
Please, Sir, हम Extra Classes कर लेंगे... Sir, जाने दीजिए, Sir..

SHASHINATH
Please, Sir!

SHASHINATH
Please, Sir!

The teacher realises their sincerity and nods.. As they begin to leave Ritesh also gets up..

TEACHER
Okay.

TEACHER
ठीक है...

SHASHINATH
Lets go.

SHASHINATH
चल...

RITESH
Wait, I'm coming too.

RITESH
रुको मैं भी आता हूँ...

SHASHINATH
Come, come..

SHASHINATH
हाँ–हाँ... चल...

They walk.. SONG continues...

RAMLEELA GROUND: MORNING

Over the P.B.S. of JANTA ROCKS...

Ramleela ground – Festive atmosphere right from early morning – Thousands of people have gathered – old men, women... Yasmin reports..

YASMIN
People from every village around have walked miles to be here, with the hope that their applications and dues will be cleared. Thousands of claims have been collected. More are pouring in..

YASMIN
अम्बिकापुर के गाँव–गाँव से लोग आये हैं – मीलों पैदल चल के – इस उम्मीद में कि इनके जो Applications और Dues हैं – वो Clear होंगे... लाखों Claims गाँव–गाँव से जमा हुए हैं – और भी जमा किए जा रहे हैं...

Bulbul Singh informs to Balram Singh on phone..

BULBUL SINGH
Thousands of people are here, sir. What are your orders?

BULBUL SINGH
हज़ारों लोग जमा हो गये हैं Sir यहाँ... Sir, Sir क्या Order है Sir...

YASMIN
The 30-day ultimatum ends today. Now let us see how the Government douses the fire lit by this open challenge.

YASMIN
सरकार को दी गई 30 दिन की Notice आज पूरी हो गई है – देखना ये है कि सरकार जनता के इस Open Challenge की आग़ को कैसे बुझा पाती है...

SECRETARIAT: MORNING

Cabinet – Kalikant Babu and C.M. worried... Balram Singh says –

BALRAM SINGH
I have a fire brigade.

BALRAM SINGH
Fire Brigade है हमारे पास...

Kalikant Babu tries to warn him..

KALIKANT BABU
Look, Mr. Balram you...

KALIKANT BABU
देखिए बलराम बाबू... आप –

Balram Singh stops him..

BALRAM SINGH
It's my district, I'll deal with it.

BALRAM SINGH
हमारा जिला है... हम कर लेंगे Handle..

RAMLEELA GROUND: MORNING

The ground is fully packed.. On the stage huge bundles of applications are stacked. Manav, Arjun, Indtrojeet, Sumitra and other key members stand on the stage looking triumphant and happy.

Dwarka takes the mike signaling the people to quieten down..

DWARKA
Today, the people have shown the government that truly 'The Public Rocks'! People roar..

DWARKA
आज... जनता ने इस सरकार को बता दिया... कि सचमुच Janata Rocks!!

CROWD
Dadu Rocks!!!

CROWD
दादू Rocks!!!

POLICE STATION-INT: MORNING

Durgalal gets the call. The constable tells him...

CONSTABLE
Sir, the Police Superintendent...

CONSTABLE
Sir, S.P. साहेब का Phone है...

Durgalal takes the phone..

DURGALAL
Jai Hind, Sir.

DURGALAL
जय हिन्द Sir.

S.P. *(on Phone)*
Go with your entire force to the ground!

S.P. *(on Phone)*
अपने पूरे Force को लेकर फ़ौरन निकलो रामलीला मैदान के लिए...

DURGALAL
Sir, I was there this morning. The situation is calm.

DURGALAL
Sir, हम Morning में हो के आये थे वहाँ से... शांति से चल रहा है Sir सब...

S.P.
Dont talk rubbish, Durgalal. Just do as you're told.

S.P.
फ़ालतू बात मत करो दुर्गालाल... जो Order मिला है उसे Follow करो...

Disconnects the phone.. Shakes his head..

DURGALAL
Sir!
(puts the phone)
I can't understand how they're always upto something.

DURGALAL
Sir...
(puts the phone)
समझ के बाहर हैं स्साले... हर Time game खेलते रहते हैं ये लोग... चलो...

RAMLEELA GROUND: MORNING

Suddenly Dwarka and others on the stage notice Police trucks arriving at all sides of the Maidan.. Yasmin trains her Camera.. Arjun steps forward to Manav..

ARJUN
What are the cops doing here?

ARJUN
ये पुलिस यहाँ क्या कर रही है?!

DWARKA
On behalf of the people, we're going to present these 384000 applications to the government.

DWARKA
हम... हम... हम ये... तीन लाख चौरासी हज़ार... और लगातार बढ़ते हुए Documents के Bundles... एक साथ...जनता की तरफ़ से... सरकार को सौंपने जा रहे हैं...

In quietly timed moves, the cops swiftly get off their vehicles and take position, with their shields and lathis ready. It is a pre-planned move. Manav notices with alarm. He leans towards Arjun..

In the crowd, Balram Singh's man Bulbul Singh, slightly disguised and surrounded by his men, gets a call.. The caller is Balram Singh..

BULBUL SINGH *(On phone)*
Sir...

BULBUL SINGH *(On phone)*
Sir...

BALRAM SINGH *(On phone)*
I want no mistake!

BALRAM SINGH *(On phone)*
चूक नहीं होना चाहिए बुलबुल...

BULBUL SINGH
Our men are in position, sir. Not to worry

BULBUL SINGH
हर कोना में अपना लोग Position में हैं Sir... फिकर Not...

BALRAM SINGH
Okay.

BALRAM SINGH
अच्छा...

And then, things happen in a flurry.

Abruptly and loudly, some groups on the edge of the Maidan begin to shout Anti-Government and Anti-Police slogans..

Dwarka pleads..

DWARKA
Please be calm. We will go about our task peacefully.

DWARKA
देखिए... शांति व्यवस्था बनाये रखिये... शांत... देखिये... शांति व्यवस्था बनाये रखिये... हमें अपना काम करना है...

MANAV *(whispering)*
So many policemen?

MANAV *(whispering)*
इतनी सारी पुलिस?

ARJUN *(smiles)*
Looks like Balram Singh is really scared.

ARJUN *(smiles)*
लगता है बलराम सिंह डर गया...

But, Manav is frowning with apprehension. Shakes his head, distracted by worry..

MANAV
No, something's wrong.

MANAV
नहीं... कुछ गड़बड़ है...

DWARKA
Please, maintain peace!

DWARKA
देखिए शांत... शांत रहें...

Bulbul Singh nods. And suddenly, his goons start hurling stones at the policemen...

Manav and Arjun both notice Bulbul at the same time and lunge at him.

MANAV *(shouts)*
Stop!

MANAV *(shouts)*
Stop!

But, it is too late. As stones fly at the cops, the police officer gives the command.

POLICE OFFICER
Charge! Clear the ground. Charge!

POLICE OFFICER
Charge करिए इन पर... हटाओ इन लोगों को यहाँ से... लाठी Charge!!!...

And, there is mayhem! The cops just charge into the bewildered crowd raining blows blindly.

Manav tries to stop the violence.

DURGALAL
Arrest him.

DURGALAL
Arrest him... पकड़ो इसे...

Manav gets hold of Bulbul and drags him to the Cops.. Yasmin tries to shoot that buit a cop snatches her camera..

DURGALAL
No.. You cannot shoot...

DURGALAL
No.. You cannot shoot...

Suddenly Commandos appear and bundle Manav in a van.. Yasmin screams –

YASMIN
Where are you taking him?

YASMIN
कहाँ ले जा रहे हैं आप लोग...

She runs after the van but the van speeds off..

Lathi charge – Water jets – People are chased away- Sumitra continues to hold Dwarka as Cops and goons hurl the bundles of applications off stage and set fire to them.. In a matter of minutes the Maidan resembles a deserted battle field..

A stunned Dwarka and Sumitra are left alone on the stage.

NATIONAL HIGHWAY/

AN ISOLATED RAILWAY CROSSING: EARLY MORNING

BALRAM SINGH
Mr. Manav Raghvendra! Do you think I'm a wedding drum? You beat it, and I dance! Very bad.
(chuckles)
You've caused enough trouble. Now, get the hell out of here! And don't even think of coming back. You see, I've exposed your reality before the people. And, the Ambikapur public doesn't spare traitors!

BALRAM SINGH
Mr. Manav Raghvendra... क्या समझ रक्खा है आपने हमको... ऍं... बाराती का ढोल... कि आप बजाते रहेंगे और हम Dance करते रहेंगे... सारा Fraud करके Business करने वाले Champion आप... अब यहाँ आ गये Corruption के ख़िलाफ़ गाँधीगीरी करने... Very Bad!... Very Bad!!...
(chuckles)
बहुत बर्बाद कर दिया आपने हमारे जिल्ला को... बस Out हो जाइए यहाँ से... औ लौटने का सोचना भी मत... काहे से कि आपके असलियत का पिटारा हम खोल दिए हैं... सबके सामने... अऽ... अम्बिकापुर की Public दग़ाबाज़ों को चलने के लायक नहीं छोड़ती...

Manav counters him silently with his cold look –

BALRAM SINGH
So, you'd better cross this line on your two feet. Or else, you'll have to be carried out. In a crate.

BALRAM SINGH
इसलिए बेहतर होगा... कि खुद ही Cross कर जाओ – ये Railway line... Walking करते करते... नहीं तो Next time Flat Position में Departure होगा... Parcel बना के...

Another train crosses by between them. The Minister leaves. As the train rattles by the Camera closes on Manav's face..

RAMLEELA GROUND: DAY

Yasmin observes with tears in her eyes, the left over burnt debris of Ambikapur's hopes.

AMBIKAPUR STREETS: DAY

Yasmin drives through streets – and through the heavy sadness that hangs in the air..

DWARKA HOUSE – INT : DAY

Yasmin's SUV stops outside Dwarka house – Sumitra receives Yasmin in the Verandah, shock writ large on her face.. Yasmin shakes her head...

Dwarka is sitting in the Living room... Coldly watching the T.V.

Over Flashing 'BREAKING NEWS' logos...

The Reporter questions –

REPORTER
The shares of Manav Raghvendra's company are consistently falling. What seems certain is that the small investor, who had put in hard-earned savings into this company, will lose the most. Billions of rupees..

REPORTER
मानव राघवेन्द्र की Company के Shares बाज़ार में लगातार लुढ़कते जा रहे हैं... ये तो पक्का है... कि आम आदमी जिसने अपनी गाढ़ी कमाई उन Shares पे Invest की है – उसको हज़ारों करोड़ का नुकसान होगा?...

SEBI SPOKESPERSON
The charges are very serious. We're investigating. Strict action will be taken against every irregularity.

SEBI SPOKESPERSON
Company पर आरोप बहुत गंभीर हैं... हम इसकी जाँच कर रहे हैं और नियम के ख़िलाफ़ कुछ पाया गया... तो सख़्त कार्रवाई होगी...

Yasmin switches channels -

Over the visuals of Manav with Sundarlal Khatri –

ANCHOR
The biggest charge against Manav Raghvendra is his connection with the political fixer, Sundarlal Khatri.
(Over Manav's pictures with Malini Mishra)
Accounts of his lavish 5-star nightlife and colourful affairs are public now. Especially with Malini Mishra. Stay tuned with us to know more about the truth behind Manav Raghavendra. We'll be back soon.

ANCHOR
सबसे बड़ा आरोप है मानव राघवेन्द्र के ख़िलाफ़... राजनीतिक गलियारों में Setting king के नाम से मशहूर सुन्दरलाल खत्री से साँठ–गाँठ का...
(Over Manav's pictures with Malini Mishra)
पाँच सितारा Night life की Life style में रंगे Mr. Manav के रंगीन संबंधों की चर्चाएँ तो आम रही हैं... उनमें से ख़ास है... मालिनी मिश्रा.. आप हमारे साथ बने रहिये... मानव राघवेन्द्र के काले–कारनामों के इस विशेष कार्यक्रम में – हम बस अभी लौटेंगे... एक छोटे से break के बाद...

Dwarka is speechless...

GANDHI CHOWK: DAY

Amidst the loud celebrations, Home Minister Balram Singh makes a grand entry into Gandhi Chowk – His party people welcome him with slogans and garlands – Bulbul Singh and Sangram Singh make sure the shopkeepers pay respect to their leader.. Balram Singh climbs on to the makeshift stage..

BULBUL SINGH
बल्लू भइया...

CROWD
Long live Balram Singh!

BULBUL SINGH
बल्लू भइया...

CROWD
Long live Balram Singh!

BULBUL SINGH
मंत्री जी...

CROWD
Long live our beloved minister!

BULBUL SINGH
मंत्री जी...

CROWD
Long live our beloved minister!

BALRAM SINGH
For a short while even I felt that this businessman from Delhi would create a revolution. That he will devise a system to clear

BULBUL SINGH
बल्लू भइया...

CROWD
जिंदाबाद...

BULBUL SINGH
बल्लू भइया...

CROWD
जिंदाबाद...

BULBUL SINGH
मंत्री जी...

CROWD
जिंदाबाद...

BULBUL SINGH
मंत्री जी...

CROWD
जिंदाबाद...

BALRAM SINGH
थोड़ा Time के लिए... हमको भी Feeling हो गया था कि कोई न कोई क्रांति तो कर ही दिखाएगा ये दिल्ली का Businessman... निकालेगा

all the government files overnight. But alas, even the fellow's computer turned out to be a stolen one!!

कोई System.. औ रातों–रात गौरमेंट (Govt.) का सब File Clear करवा देगा... अँयँ... अँयँ... मगर बेचारे का Computer ही चोरी का निकला...

BULBUL SINGH
Long live our beloved Balram Singh!

BULBUL SINGH
बल्लू भइया जिंदाबाद... बल्लू भइया जिंदाबाद... बल्लू भइया जिंद –

BALRAM SINGH
Now we'll have to wait for the CBI inquiry to know what exactly he came to loot from Ambikapur!

BALRAM SINGH
अब C.B.I. का Enquiry होगा... तब खुलासा होगा कि यहाँ अम्बिकापुर में क्या लूटने आया था...

GANDHI CHOWK / DIFFERENT LOCATIONS: DAY

Yasmin takes the people's views on the truth about Manav.

ONE MAN
The very man that we trusted turned out to be a dacoit.

ONE MAN
जिस पर भरोसा किया – वही स्साला लुटेरा निकला...

She reaches Arjun who looks angry and devastated...

ARJUN
Poor people have been taken for a ride. He has to answer for that!

ARJUN
ग़रीबों की इज्ज़त के साथ तो मज़ाक हुआ है... जवाब तो देना पड़ेगा उसको...

Yasmin sums up the story –

YASMIN
Distrust and betrayal! There's tremendous anger in the locals here. Even three days after the police action, Manav Raghvendra's whereabouts remain a mystery. Where is he? It is clear that Dwarka Anand's movement has collapsed..

YASMIN
अविश्वास... धोखा... ज़बर्दस्त गुस्सा है लोगों के बीच.. मानव राघवेन्द्र का पता Police Action के तीसरे दिन... आज भी एक रहस्य बना हुआ है... कहाँ है वो?... ज़ाहिर है – द्वारका आनन्द का खड़ा किया हुआ ये आन्दोलन... आज टूट सा गया है...

REMOTE ROAD SIDE DHABA – EXT : DAY

A bunch of Budhist Monks pass by the thatch roofed Dhaba..

Manav sits inside, looking pensive. His cell phone flashes 'Yasmin'. He doesn't even glance at it.

Just then, a convoy of cars arrive.

Raghu, Hari and his other associates get off...

Cut back into the Dhåba: Manav is signing papers after papers..

NANCY
Sir, these are the papers of your Personal accounts.

NANCY
Sir, ये सब आपके Personal accounts के Papers हैं...

RAGHU
Why are you doing this, Manav?

RAGHU
ये तू क्यूँ कर रहा है मानव?... अँ...

Manav doesn't even react..

MANAV
Tea.

MANAV
चाय...

Finally he puts in the last signature and gets up... Nanhe the Chaiwala brings tea in small galsses on a steel thali..

No one really reacts – Manav smiles –

MANAV
The tea isn't so bad, friends. I've been surviving on it the last two days.

MANAV
पी लो दोस्तों... इतनी भी बुरी नहीं है... दो दिन से जी रहा हूँ इस पे...

GANDHI CHOWK – EXT : DAY

Manav gets off an Auto rickshaw at the Gandhi Chowk – Hostile looks... He notices his blackened face on the hoarding... Begins to walk...

Youngsters from Cyber Cafe and Coaching Centres look surprised...

BOY-1
Manav Bhaiya!

BOY-1
वो मानव भइया!...

BOY-2
See, Manav Bhaiya

BOY-2
ए... वहाँ देख, मानव, मानव भइया...

BOY-3
Look, Manav Bhaiya!

BOY-3
अरे वो देख, मानव भइया!...

WOMAN
Manav!

WOMAN
अरे, ये तो मानव है!...

People curiously begin to follow him – Women rush into their balconies... windows open – bewildered and confused faces...

Manav continues to walk... a large crowd has begun to follow him – Some angry faces... Huge tension...

Bulbul Singh comes rushing out on the street - He calls up Balram Singh...

BULBUL SINGH
Greetings, sir. He's back.

BULBUL SINGH
प्रणाम Sir... वो तो लौट के आ गया Sir -

BALRAM SINGH
Who?

BALRAM SINGH
कौन?

BULBUL SINGH
The businessman from Delhi, sir.

BULBUL SINGH
वही Sir.. दिल्ली वाला –Businessman –Sir..

BALRAM SINGH
Really?

BALRAM SINGH
अच्छा!!

BULBUL SINGH
Yes, sir. Any orders?

BULBUL SINGH
Sir जी... कोई Order?

BALRAM SINGH
No. Don't do anything. The public will deal with him.

BALRAM SINGH
नईं नईं – कुछ करने की ज़रूरत नहीं है... Public खुद ही Deal करेगा उसके साथ...

A bunch of Balram Singh's party men appear – shouting slogans –

Suddenly Bulbul Singh and his men charge at Manav –

BULBUL SINGH & MEN
Beat him up!

BULBUL SINGH & MEN
मार स्साले को –

Manav's cold look stops them in their tracks. Just then Sr. S.I. Durgalal arrives –

DURGALAL
Clear off. Stop it. Nobody will break the law!

DURGALAL
हटिये... हटिये... रुको... रुको... कानून अपने हाथ में मत लो...

BULBUL SINGH
Inspector, arrest him.

BULBUL SINGH
दुर्गालाल जी... Arrest करो इसको –

Manav faces them –

MANAV
On what charge?

MANAV
किस जुर्म में?...

A SHOPKEEPER
He is a fraud! He's caused losses to the public.

A SHOPKEEPER
Fraud है स्साला... गरीब Public का नुकसान किया है...

MANAV
What fraud have I done? Who has suffered losses here?

MANAV
क्या Fraud किया है... किसका नुकसान हुआ है यहाँ...

No one says a word – Manav starts walking – The crowd follows...

DWARKA's HOUSE – EXT : DAY

As Manav arrives at Dwarka Compound – Arjun's jeep arrives to block his way –

ARJUN
After having destroyed everything, why have you come back?

ARJUN
माटी तो कर दिया सब कुछ... किस लिये आया है यहाँ...

MANAV
I'm answerable to only one man.

MANAV
मैं जवाब सिर्फ़ एक ही आदमी को दूँगा...

Manav walks into the compound... the crowd still following..

Dwarka comes out followed by Yasmin and Sumitra.. But none of them move to open the gate.

Manav walks to the platform in the community area – and stands behind the mike.

MANAV
I can understand why doors have been shut on me. I admit that I used illegitimate means in my business. They say that millions of investors of my company will lose heavily. But, I've changed everything. My company isn't worth Rs. 50 billion, but 67.13 billion. I've distributed all of that among my workers, banks and investors with profit. No one has suffered even a rupee's loss.

MANAV
हह... समझ सकता हूँ कि आज... दरवाज़े क्यूँ बन्द हैं मेरे लिए... आप सबके सामने कुबूल करना चाहता हूँ... कि मैंने अपने Business को बढ़ाने के लिए... ग़लत तरीकों का इस्तेमाल किया... अख़बारों में छपा है कि... लाखों आम लोगों का पैसा... जो मेरी Company के Shares में लगा है... डूब जायेगा... बस यही बताने लौटा हूँ... कि मैंने सब कुछ बदल दिया है... मेरी Company... जो कि... पाँच हज़ार करोड़ की नहीं... दरअसल छः हज़ार... सात सौ तेरह करोड़ की थी... वो सब मैंने अपने बैंक... अपने कर्मचारी... और Company के Share holders को मुनाफ़े के साथ बाँट दिया है... एक पैसे का नुकसान नहीं हुआ किसी का...

He looks at Arjun, Indrojeet Sen, his young brigade and the multitude of people filling every inch of the compound...

MANAV *[contd.]*
I'm left with just one thing now: A small hope that you all will forgive me.

MANAV *[contd.]*
जमा पूँजी के नाम पर... अब बस सिर्फ़ एक ही चीज़ है मेरे पास... एक छोटी सी उम्मीद... कि आप लोग मुझे माफ़ कर देंगे...

He looks at Dwarka who is still standing in the Verandah –

MANAV *[contd.]*
Uncle, I have nothing now. After losing my parents in the accident, Akhilesh gave me back my life. Then, he too left me. Now, I don't want to be orphaned for the third time. I will accept any punishment that you declare.

MANAV *[contd.]*
बाउजी... अब कुछ भी नहीं है मेरे पास... माँ–बाप को Accident में खो देने के बाद... अखिलेश ने दुबारा मुझे ज़िन्दगी दी... फिर वो भी चला गया... मैं तीसरी बार अनाथ नहीं होना चाहता... आप जो सज़ा दें – मुझे मंजूर है...

Everyone looks stunned..

The wait is palpable as Dwarka slowly comes down and joins him on the platform..

DWARKA
When the accusations were flying thick and fast, it isn't that I wasn't upset. Manav made us sad, he disappointed us. And, there will be punishment. His punishment is that he will stay here, and finish the pending task. He has given up everything and followed his conscience. For such mendicants, our doors are always open.
(People begin to clap – the youngsters look overwhelmed.)
Long live Manav! *(many times)*

DWARKA
जब एक के बाद एक आरोप... मानव पर लग रहे थे... तो ऐसा नहीं कि मुझे क्रोध नहीं आया... इसने हमें दुःख दिया... हमें मायूस किया!... और इसकी सज़ा तो मिलेगी!... और इसकी सज़ा ये है कि... अब ये यहीं रहे... जो काम बिखर गया था उसे समेटे... और पूरा करे... अपना सब कुछ त्याग के... मानव ने अपने ज़मीर की सुनी है... सोने की तपती... लंका को पार करके लौटा है ये... ऐसे फ़कीरों के लिए हमारे द्वार... हमेशा खुले रहेंगे...
(People begin to clap – the youngsters look overwhelmed.)
"मानव भैया.... जिंदाबाद!" *(many times)*

Arjun comes up on the stage and embraces Manav tearfully.

ARJUN
We couldn't understand you! But, now that you're back, we will make life hell for these corrupt fellows.

ARJUN
हम तुम्हें समझ नहीं पाये... लेकिन अब तू आ गया है मानव... अब देख कैसे Band बजाते हैं भ्रष्टाचारियों की...

As Manav embraces Dwarka, he notices Yasmin..

People roar...

PEOPLE
Long live Manav!

PEOPLE
मानव भइया... जिंदाबाद... मानव भइया... जिंदाबाद...

To everyone's surprise, Senior Inspector Durgalal steps up on stage.

S.I., DURGA LAL
Daduji, if you permit, I'd like to say something.

S.I., DURGA LAL
दादू जी... अगर आज्ञा हो तो... हम भी एक प्रार्थना करना चाहते हैं...

DWARKA
Of course.

DWARKA
हाँ ज़रूर!... आइये...

As Durgalal comes on the stage, Yasmin instructs Jolly..

YASMIN
Record this.

YASMIN
Shoot करो...

S.I., DURGALAL
Brothers, my eyes have been opened by what I witnessed here. I'm ashamed. Daduji rejects the compensation for his son's death, to start a people's movement. Manav sacrifices all his billions to protect that movement. And here, I wear this uniform to serve the goons in power. Shame on me if I serve the corrupt any longer. The austerity of truth is greater than the grandeur of lies. Daduji, please accept me as your soldier.
(He takes his cap off)
I quit the police force.

S.I., DURGALAL
भाइयों... आज जो कुछ भी हमने देखा और सुना... उससे हमारी आँखें खुल गई हैं... और शर्म आती है हमें अपने आप पर... यहाँ दादू जी... अपने बेटे के मुआवज़े के बदले... एक आन्दोलन खड़ा कर देते हैं... और मानव जी... अपने हज़ारों करोड़ रुपये न्यौछावर कर रहे हैं ताकि... आंदोलन टूटे नहीं... और हम?... हम ये खाक़ी वर्दी पहन कर... स्साला गुंडों की गुलामी करते हैं... धिक्कार है हम पर अगर... एक Minute भी और हम भ्रष्टाचार का साथ दें तो... झूठ की मलाई से... सच की भाखरी अच्छी... दादू जी... हम आपसे विनती करते हैं... आप हमें साथ लें और... सेवा का मौका दें...
(He takes his cap off)
हम इसी Time ये पुलिस की नौकरी छोड़ते हैं...

There is a stunned silence. And then a roar of approval as Dwarka embraces Durgalal..

Manav walks up to Yasmin..

MANAV
Hi.

MANAV
Hi.

Still angry, she walks away.

YASMIN
Lets go, Jolly.

YASMIN
चलो Jolly..

DWARKA HOUSE – EXT/INT: NIGHT

Later that night Manav spots Yasmin alone on the terrace... Just as he reaches the corner she has been sitting in, she picks up her book and begins to leave... He holds her hand–

MANAV
I'm Sorry!

Yasmin turns to look at him – Her face still cold...

YASMIN
But why!?

MANAV
For my irresponsible behavior.

Yasmin's face is still expressionless – cold –

YASMIN
It's okay. You are not responsible to me.

MANAV
You cannot imagine what I have gone through in these 3 days.

YASMIN
Yes, and ours were great. We had so much fun.

MANAV
I know... I know, I have hurt you!!

Yasmin cuts him sharply –

YASMIN
No, you don't! 'Hurt' has no meaning for selfish people like you.

Manav tries to hold her shoulders –

MANAV
Yasmin...

She pushes him away. And all her anger and hurt comes pouring out...

YASMIN
Damn it! With just one call from you, I abandoned a trip with the Prime Minister and rushed here. In spite of knowing everything about you, I trusted you! And you? Check your phone - 203 missed calls. You didn't answer even once?! Didn't even bother about what I must've been going through? The way they abducted you.. how worried was I! With every passing second, I would shiver with the fear that something happened to you. And, you?

MANAV
I'm Sorry!

YASMIN
But why!?

MANAV
Well, अपने ग़ैर ज़िम्मेदाराना Behaviour के लिए...

YASMIN
Its Ok... तुम्हारी मेरी तरफ़ कोई जिम्मेदारी नहीं बनती...

MANAV
यास्मिन तुम imagine भी नहीं कर सकतीं... ये ढाई दिन मैंने कैसे गुज़ारे हैं...

YASMIN
Yes... और हमारे बहुत मज़े में गुज़रे...

MANAV
I know... I know, I have hurt you!!

YASMIN
No you don't... तुम जैसे Selfish लोगों के लिए Hurt-wurt का कोई मतलब नहीं होता मानव...

MANAV
यास्मिन...

YASMIN
Damn it!... समझते क्या हो तुम!... तुमने एक Phone किया मैं Prime Minister की Trip छोड़ के चली आई... तुम्हारे बारे में सब कुछ जानते हुए भी... मैंने आँख बन्द करके तुम पर विश्वास किया... और तुम?... Check करके देखो अपने Phone को... 203 missed calls होंगे मेरे... एक बार भी Phone नहीं उठाया... एक बार भी नहीं सोचा कि मुझ पर क्या गुज़र रही होगी?... तुम्हें जिस तरह से उठा के लेके गये थे वो लोग... किस चिंता में जी रही होउँगी मैं?... हर बीतते एक पल के साथ किसी अनहोनी हादसे के ख़ौफ़ से काँप उठती थी मैं... और तुम?...

Manav suddenly holds her face and kisses her... Stunned, she pushes him away.

MANAV
I'm sorry...

MANAV
I'm sorry...

She sees the tears in his eyes –

YASMIN
Never do this to me again!

YASMIN
Never do this to me again!

He nods.

SONG fades in.

They make love..

HIGHWAY: DAWN

A vehicle stops on the highway. Manav and Durgalal get off – Durgalal points to the spot...

DURGALAL
This is where we found his body. Such a tragic accident!

DURGALAL
बस यहीं पर मिली थी उनकी Body... सचमुच, बहुत दुर्भाग्य वाली घटना थी...

Manav walks up to the spot – A big truck crosses by at the same moment – whizzing pretty close to Manav...

Manav looks away... He doesn't look convinced...

COLLECTORATE - EXT/INT: DAY

Manav and Yasmin arrive in an autorickshaw. In the Corridor Manav spots a que of people which leads into an office.. There is a table with a Clerk and a Peon sitting next to him.. It is 'जिला शिकायत कोषांग'... The Clerk throws the paper with the fifty rupee note..

CLERK
You think I'm a beggar? Here the rate is 100 bucks.

CLERK
भीखमंगा समझ रखा है क्या?... सौ रुपये Rate है यहाँ...

THE MAN
I'm in bad shape, sir. From block to district, I've appealed 9 times. But, no ration for me, no pension for my old parents. Our condition is now unbearable, sir..

THE MAN
बड़ा तकलीफ़ में हैं बाबू... Block से लेके जिला तक नौ बार आवेदन दे चुके हैं... पर ना तो राशन मिलता है... ना किरासन... और ना ही माता–पिता का वृद्धावस्था Pension.. बहुत बेहाल हैं हुजूर...

Manav picks up the application with the money. He shoves the money back into the applicant's pocket.

MANAV
Heard that? What're you demanding money for? Aren't you ashamed?

MANAV
सुन लिया आपने... किस बात के पैसे माँग रहे हैं आप?... शर्म नहीं आती आपको...

The Clerk is agitated..

CLERK
I'm helpless. Once I take this register to my superior, he'll want his share.

CLERK
क्या करें?... – ये Register लेकर अपने साहेब के पास जाएँगे... तो वो हमसे अपना Share माँगेंगे...

He notices Yasmin shooting the whole thing – Panics..

CLERK
What're you doing, madam? Please shut that.

CLERK
ये... ये क्या कर रही हैं Madam आप?... अरे इसको बन्द कीजिए...

MANAV
Then process this immediately.
(Pointing to others in the queue)
You will get no money here. From now on, no more bribes!

MANAV
तो चुपचाप ये जमा कीजिए...
(Pointing to others in the queue)
एक पैसा नहीं मिलेगा यहाँ... आज से घूस लेना–देना सब बंद!...

In the Pool Office Arjun and Sumitra argue with another official.

TARAKANT
Stop lecturing us!
(Points to his Table)
I have to pay rent for this table, understood? We too have children and families.

TARAKANT
बंद कीजिए अपना परवचन...
(Points to his Table)
इस Table का भाड़ा देना पड़ता है समझे?... अरे हम बाल–बच्चा वाले लोग हैं... परिवार वाले लोग हैं हम...

SUMITRA
Why should they pay for your illegitimate arrangements?

SUMITRA
आपके काले सौदेबाजी का दाम ये लोग क्यों चुकायें?

TARAKANT
If you behave like this, we will stop work.

TARAKANT
देखो, इस तरह से बात करोंगे तो हम काम बंद कर देंगे!

ARJUN
Do what you want, but we won't allow any corruption here.

ARJUN
अरे आपको जो करना है आप कीजिए... लेकिन घूसबाजी नहीं होने देंगे हम यहाँ...

In the Corridor, the Collector who has been informed about the goings on in his office confronts Manav and Yasmin..

D.M.
What the hell is going on here?

D.M.
What the hell is going on here?... क्या... चल क्या रहा है यहाँ पे!...

MANAV
A clean-up operation. This place has become too dirty.

MANAV
कुछ नहीं... थोड़ी बहुत सफ़ाई... गंदगी बहुत बढ़ गई है यहाँ पे...

Arjun and Sumitra have joined in – The Collector starts to call the S.P...

D.M. *(To Manav and Arjun)*
Get out of here! Or else..

D.M. *(To Manav and Arjun)*
इसी वक़्त यहाँ से बाहर निकल जाइए वर्ना –

MANAV
You'll get us arrested, right? What else can you do, Mr. Collector!

MANAV
Arrest करवा देंगे... और कर भी क्या सकते हैं आप Collector साहब...

ARJUN *(laughing)*
Perhaps you've forgotten what happened the last time you got someone arrested?

ARJUN *(laughing)*
शायद... तुम भूल रहे हो... पिछली बार किसी को अंदर किया था... तब Public ने कैसी हालत बनाई थी तुम्हारी...

MANAV
Now there shall be only one kind of action. People's direct action.

MANAV
अब सिर्फ़ एक ही Action होगा!... Public का Direct Action!

The S.P. arrives with several Cops and the D.M. shouts –

D.M.
Arrest them!!

D.M.
Arrest them!!

The Cops surround Arjun and Manav..

COP
Move.

COP
चलिए – चलिए – चलिए...

YASMIN
How can you arrest us?

YASMIN
कैसे Arrest कर रहे हैं आप लोग?...

DURGALAL
Let them go! What're you doing?

DURGALAL
अरे छोड़िए... क्या कर रहे हैं आप?...

EXTERIOR

The Police drag Manav and Arjun out of the Secretariat. A huge crowd has gathered in their support and a fervour builds up. The S.P. tries to calm down the public...

PEOPLE
Down with the Government!

PEOPLE
सरकार हाय–हाय...

S.P. *(To D.M.)*
Too many people.. Might cause a problem.
(To supporters)
Final warning: Indiscipline will not be tolerated.

S.P. *(To D.M.)*
बहुत लोग हैं... Problem हो जाएगी...
(To supporters)
आखिरी Warning दी जाती है आप लोगों को... Indiscipline बर्दाश्त नहीं होगा...

MANAV
Change your ways! Or we'll be back.

MANAV
बदल जाओ अभी भी... वर्ना हम वापस आयेंगे...

ARJUN
Everyday! Until this system improves!

ARJUN
हर रोज़ आएँगे... जब तक ये System ठीक नहीं होगा...

PEOPLE
Long live – Arjun!
Long live – Manav!

PEOPLE
अर्जुन भइया... जिंदाबाद...
मानव भइया... जिंदाबाद...

And they move...

DWARKA HOUSE/ COMMUNITY CENTRE – EXT/INT: DAY

JOURNALIST-1
Sir, we admit that the system has failed. But, are your methods right?

JOURNALIST-1
Sir, मानते हैं System fail कर गया है... ग़लत है... लेकिन क्या आपका तरीका सही है?...

DWARKA
What do you mean?

DWARKA
क्या आप... मतलब क्या है आपका?...

JOURNALIST-2
The way your people manhandled officials, threatened them.. Isn't this plain hooliganism?

JOURNALIST-2
आपके लोगों ने जिस तरह Administration का घेराव किया... और Physically उन्हें डराया... धमकाया... इसे गुण्डागर्दी नहीं तो और क्या कहेंगे...

Manav starts to speak, but Dwarka stops him.

MANAV
Well, you...

MANAV
देखिए आप –

DWARKA *(Interrupts Manav)*
One minute.
(Points to a farmer)
Please stand up.
(to media girl)
This is Nekram. His father took an agricultural loan from a public bank. It's been 7 years since they repaid it with interest. And yet, they're still making the rounds of government offices. His father passed away last year. And yet, they just can't get their land back! Now, would you like to tell us what he should do?

DWARKA *(Interrupts Manav)*
एक – एक Minute..एक Minute... येSSS...
(Points to a farmer)
इन्हें... ए... खड़े हो जाइए...
(to media girl)
ये नेकराम हैं... इनके पिता ने... खेती करने के लिए कर्ज़ा लिया था... सरकारी Bank से... सात साल हो गये... एक–एक रुपया सूद सहित लौटा दिया... चक्कर काटते रहे...Block और Collectorate के दफ़्तरों में... पिछले साल इनके पिता का देहान्त हो गया... अब घिस रहे हैं चप्पल... नेकराम जी... आप बताना चाहेंगी कि नेकराम क्या करें...

JOURNALIST-1
So, what's the plan of action?

JOURNALIST-1
तो जन सत्याग्रह समिति का आगे Action Plan क्या है?

DWARKA
The People's Satyagraha Committee has deliberated over this and has decided to place their instructions in front of the government.

DWARKA
जन सत्याग्रह समिति ने... बहुत अच्छी तरह से... इस विषय पर विचार करने के बाद... सरकार को अपना निर्देश सुनाने का फ़ैसला किया है...

JOURNALIST-2
Instructions?

JOURNALIST-2
निर्देश?

DWARKA
Yes, Instructions. In a democracy, the government functions to serve the people. Indeed, then, the people are the masters. And, masters don't plead, they command.

DWARKA
जी हाँ... निर्देश... लोकतंत्र में... सरकार जनता की सेवा के लिए बनती है... तो... जनता मालिक हुई ना... और मालिक... निर्देश देता है... माँगने का...

ARJUN
First instruction. Get rid of the Ambikapur collector.

SUMITRA
Second instruction. CBI investigation of the police action at our rally.

INDROJEET SEN
And the third instruction. Bring a law via an ordinance, which guarantees the people the right to government services.

MANAV
Approval!... Not disposal... Gone are the days when a file could be stalled. And this law be enforced immediately.

ARJUN
Within seven days.

The intellectuals are shocked.

THE MAN
Seven days!

JOURNALIST-2
How can such a vital law be implemented in just seven days?

JOURNALIST-3
Do you realize the implications of this?

MANAV *(interrupting rudely)*
If you leave it to them, it won't happen even in 700 days. If an emergency can be declared in this country within 24 hours, 7 days are more than enough for this ordinance. And there will be no compromise

Everyone is silenced..

YASMIN
So, according to you, what is the future of this country?

Manav gets up and gestures towards a young man..

MANAV
This is India's future! Ravi Kumar. Parents were labourers. The government-run school of his village was totally defunct. By painstakingly saving money, they sent him to a private school. After school, they took a loan to fund his computer training.

ARJUN
पहला निर्देश... अम्बिकापुर के Collector को फ़ौरन हटाओ...

SUMITRA
दूसरा निर्देश... रामलीला मैदान में हुए पुलिस Action की फ़ौरन – C.B.I. जाँच करवाओ...

INDROJEET SEN
और तीसरा निर्देश... Ordinance द्वारा कानून बनाओ... जनता को सरकार की सभी सेवाओं की Guarantee का अधिकार हो...

MANAV
Approval!... Not disposal... बहानेबाज़ी की Noting लिख कर... File को लटकाने का ज़माना गया!... और ये कानून... फ़ौरन लागू होना चाहिए...

ARJUN
सात दिनों के अंदर!...

THE MAN
सात दिन!

JOURNALIST-2
सात दिनों के अंदर ऐसा Important कानून कैसे बनाया जा सकता है?...

JOURNALIST-3
आप जानते हैं कि इसके कितने Implications होते हैं... और...

MANAV *(interrupting rudely)*
आप छोड़ दें... तो इनके लिए... सात सौ दिन भी कम पड़ेंगे... जब 24 घंटे में पूरे देश में Emergency लाई जा सकती है... तो इस Ordinance के लिए... सात दिन काफी हैं... और इस पर कोई Compromise नहीं होगा...

YASMIN
तो फिर इस देश का Future क्या है – आपके हिसाब से...

MANAV
ये है India का Future... रवि कुमार... मजदूरी करते थे खेतों में इनके माँ–बाप... इनके गाँव का सरकारी School.. totally defunct था... पाई–पाई जमा करके इनके माँ–बाप ने... इन्हें Private school भेजा... School pass किया... फिर Education Loan लेकर... इन्हें Computer की

Today he works in a private firm, not in the government. Salary: 40,000. Unlike his parents, he doesn't worship the government. The government is merely a service-provider to whom he pays fees, in the form of taxes. If he doesn't get service, he will stop paying. Period! This new India is telling the government and politicians to wake up! Improve your roads, power, police, hospitals, officers.. Repair your entire system! Otherwise, you have no future!

Training कराई... आज ये सरकारी नौकरी नहीं... B.P.O. की नौकरी करते हैं... चालिस हज़ार में... ये भविष्य हैं नये भारत का... जो अपने पूर्वजों की तरह... इस सरकार को अपना माई–बाप नहीं मानता... ये उस Client की तरह है... जो Payment करता है Government को Tax के रूप में... और बदले में एक अच्छी Service माँगता है... और अगर वो Service नहीं मिलती... तो ये Payment देना बन्द कर देगा... Like any other client – Period!... ये नया भारत इस सरकार और उसे चलाने वाले – Politicians से बोल रहा है कि जागो... अपने तरीके... दफ़्तर – सड़कें – बिजली... पुलिस – स्कूल – Hospital... अफ़सरान... सारे System को दुरुस्त करो... वर्ना तुम्हारा कोई Future नहीं है...

CORRIDOR – EXT: DAY

Bulbul Singh reports to Balram Singh..

BULBUL SINGH
He's going berserk, sir. Is vitiating the atmosphere in Ambikapur. Say the word, sir, and we will..

BULBUL SINGH
बहुत ही फड़फड़ा रहा है ये मानव स्साला... अम्बिकापुर का हवा बदल रहा है Sir.. आप तो Order कीजिए, बस...

BALRAM SINGH
Shut up, fool! Eager-beaver! There's nothing he can do. I have everyone's life-line in my hands.

BALRAM SINGH
चुपSS... बुड़बक कहीं का... जब देखो तब लाठी भाँजने के लिए तैयार... कुच्छ नहीं कर सकता है कोई... सबका टीक हमारे हाथ में है...

SECRETARIATE – EXT: DAY

Kalikant Babu's car is stopped by the media at the gate– He comes out and addresses them...

MEDIA GUYS
Sir.. Sir.. Sir..

MEDIA GUYS
Sir.. Sir.. Sir..

As he begins to get back into his car the Media questions –

ABP REPORTER
They've threatened complete non-co-operation. They'll stop paying taxes, and...

ABP REPORTER
Sir, उन्होंने Complete Non-Cooperation की धमकी दी है... Tax बन्द कर देंगे और...

KALIKANT BABU *(laughs)*
Whoa whoa! There are laws in this country! If those are broken, strict action will follow.

KALIKANT BABU *(laughs)*
अरे भई... अरे भई... देश में कानून है कि नहीं... अगर उसे तोड़ा गया... तो हम सख़्ती से पेश आयेंगे...

VARIOUS LOCATIONS: DY-NIGHT

It's a massive rally – Led by Dwarka, Arjun, Manav, Yasmin and Sumitra, the youth and the citizens of Ambikapur march with placards and banners –

Dwarka hands over the charter of Directions to the city S.P. and addresses –

JHANDA OONCHA RAHE HUMAARA

During the shooting of the crowd sequences, several crew members' only job was to ensure that the Indin national flag protocol was followed at all times. They were keeping a strict vigil to make sure the national flag was never put down on the crowd or handled in any inappropriate manner. At the end of the shoot, they would first collect the flags and then call pack up.

DWARKA
Please pass on these instructions of the people to the government.

DWARKA
जनता का ये निर्देश... सरकार को दे दीजिए आप...

Suddenly there is a surge and some of the youngsters push the barricades.. Immediately there is a Lathicharge – Tear gas shells and water canon jets are unleashed on the peaceful protestors.

DWARKA
Hey! What's happening! Please maintain peace. This is wrong!

DWARKA
ए... ए... अरे क्या कर रहे हो... शांत–शांत... ये ग़लत काम हो रहा है...

MANAV
Stop!

MANAV
रुक जाओ...

Led by Dwarka, Manav and Arjun the crowd faces the water canons.

Yasmin captures this mayhem and brutal police action..

Climbing on top of the Police barricade Manav thunders..

MANAV
Do what you can! Your deadline ends in 7 days.

MANAV
कर लो जो तुम लोगों को करना है... हम तुम लोगों को सात दिन का वक़्त देते हैं...

Arjun picks up from there..

ARJUN
We will not rest, until our instructions are followed. People's Movement..

ARJUN
हम ना बैठेंगे ना सोयेंगे... जब तक हमारे आदेशों का पालन नहीं हो जाता – जन सत्याग्रह...

MANAV
People's Movement!

MANAV
जन सत्याग्रह...

CABINET MEETING HALL: DAY

The Cabinet is meeting to take stock of the serious situation which has developed in Ambikapur...

C.M.
This matter is getting serious now.

C.M.
मामला Serious होता जा रहा है...

ANOTHER MINISTER
This is an open revolt! Direct attack on the Collectorate. How could the cops allow this?!

ANOTHER MINISTER
ये तो Open revolt है भाई... Collector के ऊपर Attack!... आखिर पुलिस ने इस जुलूस को Allow कैसे कर दिया...

KALIKANT BABU
Sir, perhaps the Home Minister would like to share his plan of action.

KALIKANT BABU
Sir, Home Minister शायद बताना चाहेंगे कि उनका... आगे का Plan क्या है...

C.M.
Tough action is required. The government cannot appear weak. We will..

C.M.
Tough Action की ज़रूरत है... सरकार कमज़ोर नहीं दिखनी चाहिए – हम उनको...

Balram Singh intervenes..

BALRAM SINGH
We will invite them for a discussion.

BALRAM SINGH
हम उनको बातचीत के लिए Invite करेंगे...

Surprised, C.M. and Kalikant exchange looks..

BALRAM SINGH
Mr. Kalikant, this movement has no public support. When they come for the meeting, they will be exposed.

BALRAM SINGH
अरे कालीकांत बाबू इस Group को कोई Public support नहीं है... बातचीत के लिए Invite कीजिए... सब कुछ Open हो जायेगा... औकात पता चल जायेगा...

MEETING HALL / SECRETARIAT – INT/EXT: DAY

Manav, Yasmin and Indrojeet arrive at the Secretariat –

KALIKANT BABU
Hello!

KALIKANT BABU
नमस्ते!

BALRAM SINGH
Welcome, welcome..Mr. Manav, the champion of the people's movement. One instruction after another! You seem to have taken the mickey out of us politicians!

BALRAM SINGH
Welcome - Welcome – Welcome... Mr. Manav... जन–सत्याग्रह के असली Champion – One after another निर्देश!... भई... आपने हम Politicians की हवा ही निकाल दी...

Manav gives them a cold smile. They take their seats.

KALIKANT BABU
Thank you all for coming here.

KALIKANT BABU
धन्यवाद आप सबका... यहाँ आने के लिए...

The C.M. makes a reconciliatery gesture -

C.M.
The police action on your rally was uncalled for. We are investigating it.

C.M.
परसों आपकी Rally पर जो Police Action हुआ... वो नहीं होना चाहिए था... हम उसकी जाँच करवा रहे हैं...

Balram takes over, looking at the Agenda sheet.

BALRAM SINGH
Regarding the first demand on your list..

BALRAM SINGH
आपके Agenda में जो... पहले Number पर Demand है... वो –

MANAV
Replace the Ambikapur Collector immediately.

MANAV
अम्बिकापुर के Collector को फ़ौरन बदलिये...

BALRAM SINGH
Whoa, Mr. Manav! Appointing a DM, running the administration is the government's prerogative. And the government doesn't run on your instructions.

BALRAM SINGH
अरेऽऽऽ... Manav जी... D.M. appoint करना – प्रशासन चलाना... ये सब सरकार के Power के अंदर में आता है... और सरकार आपके निर्देश के अनुसार नहीं चलती है...

Manav replies with a cold smile –

MANAV
Then why are you wasting your time by calling us here?

MANAV
तो हमको यहाँ बुलाकर... अपना Time क्यूँ ख़राब कर रहे हैं...

C.M., Kalikant Babu and Balram have a hushed argument.

C.M.
One minute, please.. Okay, we'll replace the Collector.

C.M.
एक Minute... O.K... हम Collector बदल देंगे...

Yasmin smiles and turns to Manav with admiration.

MANAV
But the new Collector will be chosen by the people.

MANAV
Thank you!... लेकिन नया Collector जनता द्वारा चुना जायेगा...

Yasmin's smile vanishes. Balram laughs -

BALRAM SINGH
Mr. Manav, Mr. Manav.. People elect leaders, not Collectors.

BALRAM SINGH
हाँऽऽ मानव जी... मानव Sir.. मानव Sir... जनता नेता चुनती है... Collector नहीं...

MANAV
Then change that system! Give us a list of five officers. People will choose one from that.

MANAV
तो अपने System को बदलिए मंत्री जी... आप पाँच Officers की List दीजिए... और हम जनता की राय से एक नाम Choose करेंगे...

Even Yasmin looks baffled.

YASMIN *(Whispers)*
Relax Manav, Don't you think you are going a bit too far!

YASMIN *(Whispers)*
Relax Manav, Don't you think you are going a bit too far!

INDROJEET
Manav, let's hear them out.

INDROJEET
मानव, सुन तो लें इनकी सोच क्या है...

Manav ignores them both..

Balram interrupts with an ingratiating smile..

BALRAM SINGH
Things are getting too heated up. Tea break?

BALRAM SINGH
बहुत गरमा–गरमी हो रही है यहाँ पर... एक Tea break हो जाये... हें!...

KALIKANT BABU
Good idea.

KALIKANT BABU
हाँ... वही ठीक रहेगा...

BALRAM SINGH
Come, please.

YASMIN
Can you calm down Manav?...

BALRAM SINGH
आइये...
(Pointing to C.M.)
Please ask for tea, sir..

Balram politely puts his arm around Manav and takes him aside –

BALRAM SINGH
No matter about the meeting. We need to speak of an important matter.

As soon as they are out of the others' earshot Balram smiles at Manav..

BALRAM SINGH
Look, Mr. Manav, this so-called Ambikapur revolution of yours will collapse like a pack of cards if I reveal that your friend, Akilesh Anand, was responsible for the flyover collapse where 7 labourers died.

Manav is stunned –

MANAV
What do you mean?!

Balram continues to smile and nod with uncanny confidence..

BALRAM SINGH
The flyover collapsed because his design was flawed.

MANAV
What rubbish! You're lying!

BALRAM SINGH
Relax, chill. I'm not saying this. The report of the expert international agency says so. I was embarrassed too. Assuming his brilliance, I put him in charge of the district's projects. Hence, I suppressed the real details of the report.

Manav's head is reeling.. Balram continues calmly..

BALRAM SINGH
अँऽ... आइये...

YASMIN
Can you calm down Manav?...

BALRAM SINGH
आइये...
(Pointing to C.M.)
ज़रा चाय बोल दीजिएगा Sir...

BALRAM SINGH
ये Meeting-Sheeting तो होती रहेगी... आइए कुछ... Important बात करते हैं... आइये...

BALRAM SINGH
देखिये मानव साहब... ये अम्बिकापुर का Revolution जो आपका है ना... वो ताश के पत्तों की तरह Frrssh करके Collapse कर जायेगा... अगर हम लोगों को ये बता दें कि Flyover कांड में सात मजदूरों और उनमें से दो परिवारों के बारह लोगों के Suicide का जिम्मेदार आपके परम प्रिय मित्र अखिलेश आनंद ही थे...

MANAV
What do you mean?!

BALRAM SINGH
Design में Fault था... Flyover उसी से तो गिरा...

MANAV
What Rubbish!.. तुम झूठ बोल रहे हो!!

BALRAM SINGH
अरे Cool down Sir.. cool down... हम थोड़ी बोल रहे हैं... Expert International Agency की Enquiry Report है हमारे पास... शर्मिन्दा तो हम खुद ही हो गये थे... कि उनको Brilliant मान के Whole District का Project In-Charge बना दिया था... इसीलिए Report का असली Detail हम दबा दिये...

BALRAM SINGH
And, dear sir, if you don't stop this circus of instructions and all, I'll make the report public. Got it?

Balram turns away from a livid Manav..

KALIKANT BABU
Come, sir. Lets resume.

BALRAM SINGH
Oh, you finished your tea, already?
(laughs)

MANAV
This meeting is over...

Manav leaves..

A stunned Yasmin and Indrojeet follow him..

ON THE HIGHWAY – CAR: DAY

In the car back to Ambikapur Yasmin is livid..

YASMIN
Why don't you say what happened?

Manav remains silent..

YASMIN
I mean, you had the people's responsibility on you. That was the government we were speaking with. But, dammit, your attitude was so autocratic! What did Balram Singh say to you?

Manav remains silent – Balram's words continue to echo in his mind..

NATIONAL HIGHWAY– OFFICE-EXT/INT: NIGHT

Durgalal puts on his Khaki dress. He drives up to the gate of the N.H. office... The watchman at the gate salutes him –

DURGALAL
A red car passed this way. Did you see it?

WATCHMAN
No sir, I did not.

Durgalal gets off his bike –

BALRAM SINGH
और मानव Sir... ये आपने... निर्देशों की नौटंकी बंद नहीं की ना... तो ये Report.. Out करना पड़ेगा हमको!... समझ गये... चलिए...

KALIKANT BABU
आइए Sir... Resume करते हैं...

BALRAM SINGH
अरे... इतनी जल्दी पी लिया Sir...यास्मिन जी...
(laughs)

MANAV
This meeting is over...

YASMIN
तुम बोल क्यों नहीं रहे हो मानव... हुआ क्या है?...

YASMIN
I mean लोगों की जिम्मेदारी थी तुम पर... हम एक सरकार से बात कर रहे थे... Damn it, Your attitude was so autocratic! आखिर क्या कह दिया है बलराम सिंह ने तुमसे...

DURGALAL
क्या भाई... यहाँ एक लाल गाड़ी गई थी... देखा है क्या?

WATCHMAN
नहीं साहब... हमने तो नहीं देखा...

DURGALAL
Who else is on duty here?

DURGALAL
यहाँ और कौन–कौन है Duty पे?...

We see a shadow in the background crossing over the wall and entering the building –

WATCHMAN
Sir, there's Ratan Singh.

WATCHMAN
साहब वो... रतन सिंह है...

DURGALAL
Call him!

DURGALAL
बुला उसको...

WATCHMAN *(Shouts)*
Ratan.

WATCHMAN *(Shouts)*
ए रतन...

DURGALAL
He'll come. Show me your log book.

DURGALAL
एऽऽ... वो आएगा... तू अपना Log book दिखा मुझे... चल...

Inside the office, in the dark, Manav downloads all of Akhilesh's files and shuts down the computer...

DWARKA HOUSE – INT: NIGHT

Manav and Yasmin go through the files on Akhilesh's computer..

MANAV
Look at this! Akki's design. And, the appreciation from National Engineers Association. Another from Pete Hubert, the American design guru. And that sonofabitch claims the design was faulty!

MANAV
ये देखो... अक्की का Design... National Engineers Association का Application Letter... और ये America के Designing गुरू... PETE HUBERT की तारीफ़... और वो स्साला बोलता है – Design Faulty था...

MANAV *[contd.]*
This here is Akki's confidential report to the Chief Minister. The work was illegally grabbed from the designated company by this Shiv Shakti. Balram's brother, Sangram Singh's company. And here, 2 days before his accident he writes that his report was leaked, and he was receiving threats. Hence, he wanted to resign.

MANAV *[contd.]*
तुमको तो मालूम है असली बात क्या है... और ये देखो... अक्की की Confidential Report... जो उसने Chief Minister को लिखी थी... Construction Company जिसको Contract दिया था – वो काम नहीं कर रही थी... उससे काम छीन लिया था... इस शिव शक्ति ने... जो बलराम सिंह के भाई... संग्राम सिंह की Company है... और ये देखो... अपनी Diary में Accident से ठीक दो दिन पहले लिखा है... उसे डर है कि उसकी Confidential Report Leak हो गई है और... उसे धमकी मिल रही है... इसी वजह से वो Resign देना चाहता था...

Yasmin looks stunned.. Manav continues..

MANAV
He was referring to this inquiry! Everyone's guilty, Yasmin. From the Chief Minister to Balram and his brother, Sangram. This entire Department.

MANAV
और इसी Enquiry का हवाला दे रहा था वो... सभी दोषी हैं यास्मिन... Chief Minister से लेकर बलराम और उसके भाई संग्राम सिंह... ये Department – सब –

YASMIN
We need to answer just one question to link it all up. Who ordered Akhilesh's death?

YASMIN
अब बस एक ही कड़ी बचती है जो Link कर सके... कि अखिलेश के हादसे को अंजाम किसने दिया?...

ROAD SIDE – BAR: NIGHT

A jeep slows down and stops close to the bar – Durgalal gets off telling Manav..

DURGALAL
Stay here, sir. I'll have a look.

DURGALAL
आप यहीं बैठिए Sir.. हम देखते हैं...

Durgalal spots Chotelal in a corner sitting alone.. his glass empty. He walks to the counter.

DURGALAL
A pint, please.

DURGALAL
एक अद्धा दे...

He sits next to Chotelal and pours liquor in his glass. Chotelal smiles..

CHOTELAL
Inspector sir!

CHOTELAL
दरोगा जी...

EARLY MORNING – BEFORE DAWN

Manav and Durgalal have taken Chotelal to the accident spot.. He is crying..

CHOTELAL
No, no, no, no. I.. I.. I didn't see anything, sir.

CHOTELAL
नहीं... नहीं... नहीं... नहीं... हमने... हमने नईं... हमने नईं... हमने नईं देखा Sir... हमने नईं... हम नईं समझ सकते...

MANAV
Watch carefully! Your bike was here. And another bike was following you. Here..

MANAV
ठीक से देखो... तुम्हारी Bike यहाँ जा रही थी... और दूसरी Bike पीछे से आ रही थी...

Manav shows him a reconstructed animation of the accident on his Tablet. Chotelal's eyes get fixed on the images on the Tablet... He starts to tremble and sputter incoherently..

CHOTELAL
No, no.. That Sangram Singh.. He'll kill me, sir. Sangram Singh will kill me! Please save me, sir.

CHOTELAL
नईं... नईं... नईं... वो... वो संग्राम सिंह... संग्राम सिंह Sir... वो हमको मार डालेगा Sir... वो संग्राम सिंह हमको मार डालेगा... हमको बचा लो सा'ब... मार डालेगा...

Manav has a seething cold look in his eyes..

KALIKANT BABU's RESIDENCE: NIGHT

Kalikant Babu looks stunned at what Manav and Yasmin have told him.

KALIKANT BABU
Where is this Chhotelal?

KALIKANT BABU
आपका ये आदमी... छोटेलाल कहाँ है?...

YASMIN
He's with us. Safe.

YASMIN
हमारे पास है... Safe है...

Kalikant nods. And then looks at Manav –

KALIKANT BABU
Sorry about the tragedy. But believe me, this report wasn't deliberately leaked from the CM's office.

KALIKANT BABU
Sorry for the tragedy... लेकिन विश्वास कीजिए कि ये Report – C.M. Office से जानबूझ कर Leak नहीं की गई होगी...

MANAV
Deliberately or otherwise; the responsibility lies with the office to which Akhilesh sent the report.

MANAV
जानबूझ कर की गई हो... या हो गयी... ज़िम्मेदारी उस Office की है... जिसे अखिलेश ने ये Report भेजी थी...

KALIKANT BABU
Yes, I understand that. But the people you refer to are also in this government. Isn't too difficult to obtain a copy of confidential papers.

KALIKANT BABU
हाँ... I understand that... But आपने जिन लोगों की बात की... वो भी सरकार में हैं... बहुत मुश्किल नहीं है ये... Confidential papers की Copy निकालना...

YASMIN
What're you trying to say?

YASMIN
आप कहना क्या चाहते हैं?...

KALIKANT BABU
Remove the CM's name from this controversy! I'll take action against Sangram Singh.

KALIKANT BABU
आप C.M. का नाम इस Controversy से हटा लीजिए... संग्राम सिंह पर कार्रवाई मैं करूँगा...

BALRAM's HOUSE - INT/EXT: DAY

Sangram Singh's birthday celebrations are in progress.

MOTHER
My son is looking so handsome today.

MOTHER
मेरा बेटा कितना सुंदर लग रहा है...

BALRAM SINGH
Greetings, greetings to all.

BALRAM SINGH
अरे प्रणाम – प्रणाम – प्रणाम... सब...

Balram Singh comes down the steps at the same time the D.G.P.'s car enters his compound... Sangram touches his feet.

SANGRAM SINGH
Brother, today I want a special gift from you!

SANGRAM SINGH
भैया... आज तो हम Special Gift ले के रहेंगे आपसे...

BALRAM SINGH
Happy birthday. Be happy!

BALRAM SINGH
Happy Birthday - मंगलमय हो...

SANGRAM SINGH
Thank you, brother, thank you.

SANGRAM SINGH
Thank you भइया जी... Thank you...

BALRAM SINGH
May you live long!

BALRAM SINGH
हज़ार साल जियो...

SANGRAM SINGH
Thank you...

SANGRAM SINGH
Thank you...

The D.G.P. and some Sr. Cops enter the house and salute the Home Minister...

BALRAM SINGH
Welcome, welcome, DGP. Even you have come to say Happy Birthday!

BALRAM SINGH
आइये आइये आइये... DGP Sahab!... लगता है आप भी Happy Birthday बोलने आ गये!

The D.G.P. looks a bit embarrassed and uncomfortable...He hands over a document to Balram..

BALRAM SINGH
What's this? A gift!?

BALRAM SINGH
ये क्या है?... Gift!...

D.G.P.
Arrest warrant for Sangram Singh!

D.G.P.
संग्राम सिंह के नाम Arrest Warrant है...

MOTHER
Warrant!

MOTHER
Warrant!

SANGRAM SINGH
What's the charge?

SANGRAM SINGH
एऽऽ... Charge का है?

D.G.P.
Murder! Of engineer Akhilesh Anand.

D.G.P.
302.. Engineer Akhilesh Anand के Murder का Charge...

SANGRAM SINGH
What nonsense! The police inquiry cleared me.

SANGRAM SINGH
क्या बकवास है – Police enquiry में सब Clear हो गया है...

Balram stops him...

BALRAM SINGH
It's the court's warrant, Sangram. They've bypassed the police. Go with them. This is your special birthday gift.

BALRAM SINGH
Court का Issue किया हुआ Warrant है संग्राम... Police को ही Bypass कर गये हैं... चलिए, जाइए... आज यही है आपका Special Birthday Gift..हें...

As the Cops move – Sangram's mother and wife begin to cry..

MOTHER
Today is his birthday! At least today...

MOTHER
बेटा आज तो इसका जन्मदिन है... कम से कम आज तो –

BALRAM SINGH *(To his mother)*
Enough, Ma. Be quiet.

BALRAM SINGH *(To his mother)*
अम्मा, बस – बस... चुप रहिये...

A bitter Balram Singh takes the D.G.P. aside, as his men escort Sangram Singh out..

PARTY WORKER
Love live Sangram Singh!

PARTY WORKER
संग्राम सिंह जिंदाबाद!!!

BALRAM SINGH
Who is behind this?

BALRAM SINGH
कौन है इसके पीछे?

He doesn't have to wait for an answer. Surrounded by Arjun's deadly looking men, Ajay steps forward. They look into each other's eyes for a long, tense moment. And then Balram smiles menacingly.

HIGHWAY – AKHILESH's ACCIDENT SITE: EVENING

The Sun is about to set when an autorickshaw stops on the highway. Dwarka gets off wearing a broken look.

For the first time he is unable to control his grief and as he bends down going on his knees – caressing the tarmac, he breaks down... A truck passes by on the road... its sound hurtling the images and Dwarka howls as he feels the ground with his hands...

Manav and Yasmin arrive. Yasmin moves towards him but Manav stops her. Arjun and Sumitra too reach the spot. And soon a huge crowd gathers. Arjun and Sumitra hold the old man's shoulders. But nothing can console him at this moment..

Hundreds of people arrive. And all of them sit on the highway against the setting sun, lighting candles in memory of Akhilesh Anand..

SECRETARIAT / MEDIA POINT: DAY

The Media is in full force as the C.M. with Balram Singh walks upto the podium..

MEDIA
Mr. Chief Minister. The Home Minister's brother is in the dock. It's the government's moral responsibility..

MEDIA
मुख्यमंत्री जी, खुद Home Minister के भाई पर आरोप लगे हैं... आपकी सरकार नैतिक जिम्मेवारी लेते हुए...

An irritated C.M. intervenes..

C.M.
So, Balram Singh accepted the moral responsibility! He handed over his innocent brother to the cops on his birthday! What more do you want?

C.M.
नैतिक जिम्मेवारी तो ली ना बलराम जी ने... तभी तो पुलिस के आते अपने निर्दोष भाई को... उसके जन्मदिन पर... पुलिस को सौंप दिया... अरे और क्या चाहते हैं आप लोग?

MEDIA
Today is the last day of the deadline issued by the People's Movement! Your government...

MEDIA
जन सत्याग्रह के निर्देशों को पालन करने का आज आखिरी दिन है... और आपकी सरकार ने...

The C.M. looks at Balram Singh who signals him to continue..

C.M.
Look, our stand is clear. Very respectfully, we invited them for a meeting. But, their attitude was dictatorial. The people of Ambikapur have have been brainwashed by these so-called activists. The government is run by people's representatives, not by mobs!

C.M.
देखिये... हमारा Stand आज भी वही है... हमने आदर सम्मान से उन्हें बातचीत करने के लिए बुलाया था... लेकिन उनका Attitude, Dictator जैसा... अम्बिकापुर के लोगों का Brainwash कर दिया है इन So called... 'जन–सत्याग्राहियों' ने... राज जनता के प्रतिनिधियों से चलता है... हुड़दंग से नहीं...

DWARKA HOUSE/ COMMUNITY CENTRE- EXT: DAY

The place is buzzing with excitement – All the Core Committee Members are there in full force... The media is covering every word being spoken...

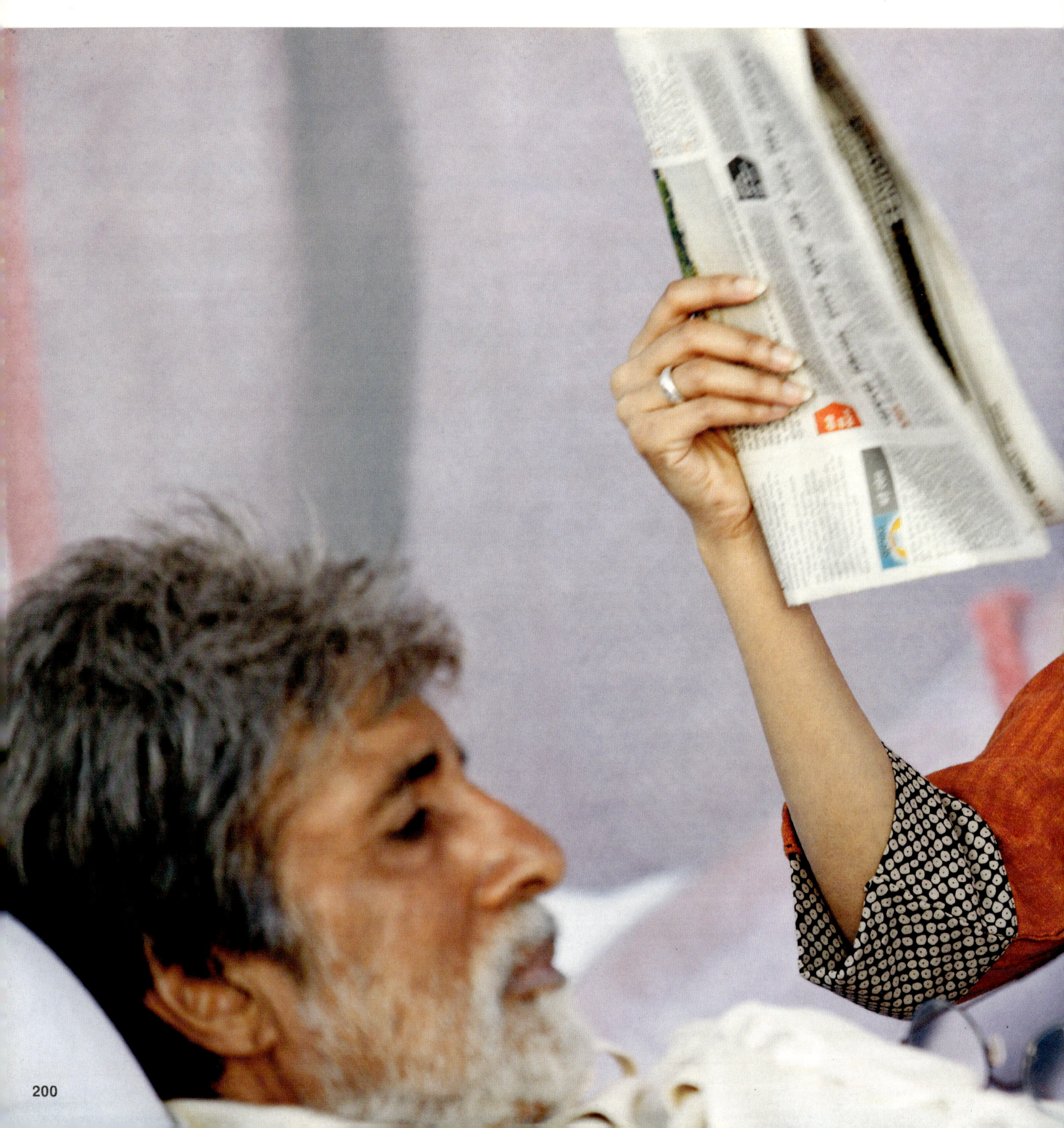

We all need a little bit of fan!

Amrita Rao was ragged thoroughly by the other senior actors. During the fast sequence Arjun and Ajay noticed how when she had to fan Mr. Bachchan with a newspaper, with all the sincerity on her face, she was fanning herself more than she was fanning him! Everyone teased her to death about it!

GANGA
Right here... below...

GANGA
य...यहीं... हैं... नीचे हैं...

DWARKA
Call them.

DWARKA
बुलाओ...

GANGA
Come here..

GANGA
आ...आओ...

DWARKA
Come, sit next to me.

DWARKA
तू इधर आ... बैठ... और आगे आ... और आगे...

The woman sits near him as her kids come and join her – Dwarka smiles at them –

DWARKA
Okay, if you insist, I will eat. But, you'll have to guarantee me one thing.

DWARKA
ठीक है... तू कहती है तो... मैं रोटी खा लेता हूँ... लेकिन... एक बात की... Guarantee देनी होगी तुझे...

Everyone is surprised, as is the woman...

DWARKA
Henceforth, your kids will never sleep hungry. Give me that guarantee, and I'll eat right now.

DWARKA
कि आज के बाद ये... तेरे दोनों बच्चे... कभी भी... भूखे नहीं सोएँगे... तू Guarantee दे... मैं भी रोटी खा लूँगा तेरी...

The woman understands the import of Dwarka's words and begins to cry –

GANGA
How can I...?

GANGA
मैं ये...

DWARKA
Precisely! That's why we are on a hunger-strike. So that our children never have to sleep hungry.

DWARKA
इसीलिए... इसी के लिए हम... सब ये अनशन कर रहे हैं... ताकि हमारी संतानें... कभी भी भूखी ना सोयें...

Evening has set in – Dwarka gestures to everyone to come and sit near him.

DWARKA
As time goes on, I may become unconscious. If that happens, do not try to revive me medically.

DWARKA
आओ... बैठो–बैठो... दिन चलते... मेरा ये शरीर... बेहोशी के आलम में जा सकता है... यदि ऐसा हुआ तो... मुझे Medically revive करने की कोशिश मत करना...

MANAV
Uncle, I think we will be...

MANAV
बाउजी, मुझे लगता है हम कोई –

DWARKA *(Cutting in)*
Promise me, you will fulfill my instruction. You won't stop me. No matter what.

DWARKA *(Cutting in)*
ये... तुम सबका वादा है... मेरे निर्देश का पालन करोगे... मुझे रोकोगे नहीं... किसी भी हाल में...

A little boy and his sister begin to sing.

Everyone joins in.

RAMLEELA GROUNDS/ C.M.'s ROOM: LATE AFTERNOON

Hundreds of children from different schools have come to see Dwarka – Sumitra comes up to Dwarka...

KIDS *(at once)*
Daduji... Daduji...

KIDS *(at once)*
दादू जी... दादू जी...

SUMITRA
Dad.. Dad.. so many children have come to see you.

SUMITRA
बाबूजी... बाबूजी... ढेर सारे बच्चे आये हैं आपसे मिलने...

Indrojeet Sen hands Dwarka his Spectacles..

INDROJEET SEN
Here.

INDROJEET SEN
ये लीजिए...

Dwarka begins to get up with a lot of help –

The children erupt in glee as they see Dadu who waves at them... The kids suddenly pull a mask of Dwarka's face from their back and wear it all at the same time –

In a flash, the ground is full of Dwarka's masks...

KIDS *(at once)*
Daduji... Daduji...

KIDS *(at once)*
दादू जी... दादू जी...

He then takes the microphone.

DWARKA
Children..

DWARKA
बच्चों... मैं...

EVERYONE
Daduji...

EVERYONE
दादूजी...

KIDS *(at once)*
Daduji...

KIDS *(at once)*
दादू जी...

Suddenly Dwarka is unable to balance his weight on his feet – and drops on the floor...

They all run to carry him back to his cot –

The whole crowd gasps some of the children begin to cry...

A graphic social media montage continues, urging Manav to do something.

AN ISOLATED SPOT: EXT. EVENING

Gauri Shankar and his men are waiting – Manav arrives with Durgalal and Indrojeet Sen.

GAURI SHANKAR
Greetings, Mr. Manav. We were always keen to join you. But, you..

GAURI SHANKAR
नमस्कार, मानव भाई... अरे हम तो आपके साथ शुरू से ही जुड़ना चाहते थे लेकिन... आपने...

MANAV
Never mind then. Today, I want to help you.

MANAV
तब की बात छोड़िए... आज हम आपकी मदद करने आये हैं...

Gauri Shankar is surprised...

GAURI SHANKAR
I don't understand...

GAURI SHANKAR
मैं समझा नहीं...

MANAV
But I can understand. In spite of such a massive movement against the government, why is the main opposition party not exploiting that?

MANAV
लेकिन मैं समझ सकता हूँ... कि सरकार के सामने इतना बड़ा जन–सत्याग्रह खड़ा हो जाये तो भी Main opposition Party उसका फ़ायदा क्यूँ नहीं उठा पा रही है...

GAURI SHANKAR
Our support is yours!

GAURI SHANKAR
आप हमारा Support done मानिए...

MANAV
But only from outside.

MANAV
लेकिन सिर्फ़ बाहर से...

Gauri Shankar smiles –

GAURI SHANKAR
What is this, Mr. Manav! This is like getting married without pleasure of love! We will join with you not just in statements, but also on the ground. Only then will the government move!

GAURI SHANKAR
अरे क्या मानव भाई... अब ऐसा भी मत करो आप कि हम अपनी जात भी गँवा दें – और भात भी ना खायें... एँ... अरे हम आपके साथ लड़ेंगे तो सिर्फ़ विचारों से नहीं... ज़मीन पे भी आपके साथ रहेंगे... सरकार तो तभी हिलेगी...

RAMLEELA GROUND – BACK STAGE: MORNING

'Bhartiya Mukti Dal' Party workers enter the Ramleela Ground cheering...

Yasmin finds Manav with Arjun and Indrojeet Sen –

YASMIN
So, this was the deal you struck last night! Now, this fundamentalist party will run our movement?

YASMIN
तो ये समझौता किया तुमने कल रात को... अब ये कट्टरवादी Party चलाएगी हमारे आंदोलन को...

MANAV
C'mon, Yasmin. Don't overreact. Our movement needs support now. I don't care where it comes from!

MANAV
Come on Yasmin, Overreact मत करो... जन–सत्याग्रह को अभी Support की ज़रूरत है... कहीं से भी मिले, मैं ले लूँगा! –

YASMIN
Manav, they play the politics of communalism and hatred. They'll hijack the whole movement. And, wear the crown of victory as well.

YASMIN
मानव ये लोग समाज को बाँटने की राजनीति खेलते हैं... They'll hijack the whole movement - और जीत का ताज अपने सर पर पहन लेंगे...

Arjun joins in –

ARJUN
But, we won't let that happen. It will be the people's victory.

ARJUN
लेकिन हम ऐसा होने नहीं देंगे... जीत पूरी जनता की ही होगी...

MANAV
Moreover, what difference does credit make.

MANAV
और ताज का Credit किसी को भी मिले... क्या फ़र्क पड़ता है...

YASMIN
Big difference, Manav! Remember for us the means are as important as the end.

YASMIN
पड़ता है मानव!... याद रखना... हम जिस रास्ते को अपनाते हैं... वो उतना ही Important है जितनी हमारी मंज़िल...

Manav sounds sharp –

MANAV
Why don't you say this to that woman who sends her kids to bed hungry every night? Or to my friend, Akhilesh, who lost his life?

MANAV
ये तुम उस औरत को जा के क्यूँ नहीं बता देतीं... जो रोज अपने बच्चों को भूखा सुला देती है... या मेरे दोस्त अखिलेश को... जो अपनी जान गँवा बैठा...

YASMIN
You can't get emotional and make judgments.

YASMIN
तुम भावना में बह के अपने Judgements नहीं ले सकते मानव –

MANAV
Why not? I joined this movement only for emotional reasons. For this stubborn old man, who is sacrificing his life because of an uncaring government.

MANAV
Why not?... मैं इस Movement में सिर्फ़ भावनाओं की वजह से जुड़ा हुआ हूँ... इस... इस बूढ़े ज़िद्दी आदमी के लिए... जो एक बेपरवाह Government की वजह से... अपनी जान दे रहा है...

YASMIN
And you think he'd approve of these fundamentalists?

YASMIN
और तुम सोचते हो इन कट्टरवादियों का साथ उन्हें मंजूर है?

MANAV
Look, that's my responsibility, okay? I'll do whatever it takes to end his fast.

MANAV
Listen, ये मेरी जिम्मेदारी है... इनका अनशन तोड़ने के लिए मुझे जो भी करना पड़े... मैं करूँगा...

BALRAM SINGH HOUSE: INT. EARLY MORNING

Balram turns the TV on – It's Gauri Shankar giving a statement...

GAURI SHANKAR *(On TV)*
If they don't have the guts to pass the Ordinance, call for an emergency session of the Assembly. We'll support it. People's instructions should be followed. People are the rulers. Not obeying them is an insult of democracy.

GAURI SHANKAR *(On TV)*
अरे Ordinance लाने का Guts नहीं है... तो Special Emergency session बुलाइए... हम समर्थन करेंगे... जनता के निर्देशों का पालन होगा... सही मायने में... जनता ही राजा है... उसके आदेशों का पालन ना करना... लोकतंत्र का अपमान है...

Balram's face becomes bitter...

BALRAM SINGH
Really?!

BALRAM SINGH
अच्छा!!!

SECRETARIAT – EXT/INT – BALRAM SINGH's OFFICE:DAY

Gauri Shankar furiously walks into Balram Singh office – Flashing a Notice...

GAURI SHANKAR
What is this, Mr. Balram! You are cancelling my bridge-contract without a notice!

GAURI SHANKAR
क्या बलराम बाबू... बिना Notice दिये आप हमारे पुल का Contract cancel कर रहे हैं –

Balram gets up to receive him-

BALRAM SINGH
Mr. Gauri, relax.. Chill. Please sit. The notice is simply since the work wasn't completed in time.

BALRAM SINGH
अरे गौरी भाई बैठिए–बैठिए... काहे आप Fire हो रहे हैं... Please sit down... अरे... क्या है कि काम Time frame में Complete नहीं हुआ ना ये उसी का Notice है...

GAURI SHANKAR
Whose work is ever completed in time, tell me.

GAURI SHANKAR
अरे आज तक किसका काम Time frame में complete हुआ है बताइये आप...

BALRAM SINGH
With this excuse, we got to meet at least. What'll you have: tea or coffee??

BALRAM SINGH
अच्छा चलिए इसी बहाने आपसे मिलना हो गया... क्या लीजिएगा... चाय कि Coffee?

GAURI SHANKAR
First take the notice back.

GAURI SHANKAR
पहले Notice Return लीजिए आप...

Balram takes the notice..

BALRAM SINGH
Ok taken. Sit down. Tea or coffee?

BALRAM SINGH
चलिए ले लिया... Sit down... चाय कि Coffee?

Gauri Shankar sits down.

GAURI SHANKAR
Coffee.

GAURI SHANKAR
Coffee मँगाइए...

BALRAM SINGH *(Orders to Attendant)*
Hey...

BALRAM SINGH *(Orders to Attendant)*
ए...

BALRAM SINGH
This is your file, personal as well as business. So many complaints about projects, scams. Fit for CBI. But, I've

BALRAM SINGH
ये आप ही का File सब है... Personal और Business भी... तरह–तरह का Complain.. Project सब में घपला का Case बना के रखा है

suppressed everything. You won't get a single notice. Rest in peace.

Department का लोग... Fit for C.B.I... हमने सब रोकवा दिया... Not a single notice जायेगा आपको... Rest in Peace...

GAURI SHANKAR
Where am I speaking against you either?

GAURI SHANKAR
हम कहाँ कुछ बोल रहे हैं...

BALRAM SINGH
I trust you. No one wants to dissolve the govt. Everyone from the CM downwards has their project-investments in the pipeline. They'll all come to nought.
(Pointing to the files-)
You will go bankrupt!

BALRAM SINGH
भरोसा है आप पर... सरकार कौन गिराना चाहता है... अरे C.M. से लेकर Down the line सबका Project Investment फँसा हुआ है... सब गुड़ गोबर हो जायेगा...
(Pointing to the files-)
आप तो बरबाद ही हो जायेंगे –

GAURI SHANKAR
I have always cooperated with you. But, your alliance partners? How will you shut them up?

GAURI SHANKAR
अरे हम तो आपको हमेशा से Co-operate करते आये हैं... लेकिन... आपके जो गठबंधन के नेता हैं... उनको आप कैसे Shutup कराइगा...

Balram laughs –

BALRAM SINGH
I shall request them. They will be managed. You know me.
(Laughs)
Right?

BALRAM SINGH
Request कर लेंगे... Management तो करना पड़ेगा ना... आप तो जानते ही हैं हमको...
(Laughs)
है कि नहीं...

OPPOSITION PARTY H.Q.– EXT - DAY

Gauri Shankar is surrounded by his party workers as he addresses the Media -

MEDIA
Mr. Gauri Shankar, why have you withdrawn your support to the Jan Satyagraha movement?

MEDIA
गौरी शंकर जी, जन सत्याग्रह आंदोलन से आपने Support क्यों वापस ले लिया?...

GAURI SHANKAR
Look, look. I always support the people. However, laws can only be made in the Assembly. They can't happen on the streets now, can they?

GAURI SHANKAR
देखिए... देखिए... जनता के हित में कोई भी बात हो... उसे हमारा पूरा समर्थन है... लेकिन जो कानून है... वो तो विधान सभा में ही बनता है ना... उसको आप सड़क पर थोड़ी बना सकते हैं...

RAMLEELA GROUND –INT/ EXT – MORNING/ EVENING

Manav looks troubled, having just learnt about Gauri Shankar's withdrawal of support.

A little later, Yasmin gets a call -

YASMIN
Hello Mr.Kalikant.

YASMIN
नमस्ते, कालीकांत बाबू...

Kalikant gets to the point without preamble…

KALIKANT *(Tense)*
Yasmin, can you put an end to Dwarka Anand's hunger strike?

KALIKANT *(Tense)*
यास्मिन, ये द्वारका आनन्द का अनशन तुम तुड़वा सकती हो?

YASMIN
I don't understand... He has very clearly stated that until the people's...

YASMIN
मैं समझी नहीं... उन्होंने साफ़ कह दिया था कि जब तक... जनता के निर्देश –

KALIKANT *(raised voice, agitated)*
Look, can you end it or not?

KALIKANT *(raised voice, agitated)*
देखो तुम तुड़वा सकती हो या नहीं?...

Yasmin is stunned at his desperate tone..

YASMIN *(quietly)*
Not till you fulfill the demands of the people. No.

YASMIN *(quietly)*
जब तक आप जनता के निर्देशों का पालन नहीं करते... नहीं...

She disconnects the phone.

RAMLEELA GROUND -EXT - MORNING

Early in the morning, a letter arrives from the government.

INDROJEET SEN
We've received the letter.

INDROJEET SEN
ये Letter आया है...

SUMITRA
Dad, Mr. Indrojeet has come..

SUMITRA
बाबूजी... इन्द्रजीत जी आये हैं...

INDROJEET SEN
Daduji...

INDROJEET SEN
दादूजी...

DWARKA *(Handing letter to Yasmin)*
Read it aloud.

DWARKA *(Handing letter to Yasmin)*
क्या है ये इसको पढ़ो...

YASMIN
The Government has called us to discuss our demands. And they request you to end your fast.

YASMIN
हमारी माँगों पर सरकार हमसे बातचीत करना चाहती है.... और आपसे अनशन तोड़ने का Request किया है...

MANAV
Uncle, nothing will make everyone happier than you breaking your fast.

MANAV
बाबूजी आप अनशन तोड़ दें... इससे बड़ी खुशी की बात और क्या हो सकती है...

SECRETARIAT: INT: AFTERNOON

It's a tense meeting.

KALIKANT
See..

ARJUN
Enough of politics, sir. Please get to the point.

KALIKANT
We're ready to discuss every point. But break your fast, please..

MANAV
You bring in the ordinance. The fast will break by itself.

THE OTHER MINISTER
Without the cabinet's approval, the ordinance can't..

Kalikant cuts him sharply...

KALIKANT
I have the CM's approval.
(To Manav)
I give you my personal guarantee that the govt will bring in the ordinance. It'll take a short while. Please get Daduji to end his fast. Manav and Arjun look at each other...

KALIKANT
Let's address the media together.

Balram Singh enters, smiling with surprise.

BALRAM SINGH
Wow! A terrific party is going on! But, you forgot to invite me.

Kalikant looks irritated and nervous..

KALIKANT
Mr. Balram, this meeting was called in a hurry.

BALRAM SINGH
Mr. Kalikant, I hope the hurry doesn't untie the cords of our alliance.

KALIKANT
These are difficult times, Mr. Balram. We need patience and an attitude of compromise.

BALRAM SINGH
Compromise!? With these blackmailers? Mister Dadu's fast is just a big farce..

KALIKANT
देखिए...

ARJUN
राजनीति बहुत हो गया Sir... अब सीधे Point पर आइए...

KALIKANT
हर Point पर चर्चा करने के लिए तैयार हैं हम... बस आप अनशन तुड़वाइए...

MANAV
आप Ordinance ले आइए... अनशन अपने आप टूट जायेगा...

THE OTHER MINISTER
Ordinance तो भाई बिना Cabinet के...

KALIKANT
मुख्यमंत्री की सहमति ले चुका हूँ मैं...
(To Manav)
मैं आपको Personal guarantee देता हूँ – सरकार Ordinance लाएगी... थोड़ा वक़्त लग सकता है... बस, आप... दादूजी का अनशन तोड़वाइए...
I have the CM's approval.

KALIKANT
आइए, Media से मिलकर बात कर लेते हैं!...

BALRAM SINGH
अरे वाह!... बड़ा ज़बर्दस्त Party चल रहा है यहाँ... क्या कालीकांत बाबू... हमको Invite करना ही भूल गये!...

KALIKANT
बलराम बाबू, थोड़ा जल्दी में Meeting बुलाना पड़ा...

BALRAM SINGH
कालीकांत बाबू... देखिए, जल्दबाजी में कहीं गठबंधन का गाँठ ही न खुल जायें...

KALIKANT
बलराम बाबू, कठिन समय है... कुछ Solution निकाल कर समझौता करें हम लोग...

BALRAM SINGH
समझौता?... Blackmailer लोगों के साथ!!... येऽऽ Total ड्रामेबाजी है Mister Dadu का अनशन...

Arjun gets enraged and threatens Balram.

ARJUN
Hey!!

BALRAM SINGH
Whoa!

ARJUN
Don't you dare utter a word against Daduji!

Kalikant tries to calm the situation down...

BALRAM SINGH *(Cool as a cucumber)*
See that? See that?

KALIKANT
Please, please. Don't get heated up.

BALRAM SINGH
Have a look! The violence of peaceful activists!

ARJUN
I'll show you some violence!

Manav restrains him with his right hand...

Balram Singh smiles..

BALRAM SINGH
Calm down. Jump and dance as much as you want! This coalition government can't make any law without my consent.

Manav walks up and comes directly face to face with Balram Singh..

MANAV
The law will be made, Balram Singh! Because the youth of today has seen through criminal politicians like you. And, forget the cords of the alliance. Your pyjama cords will be opened to strip you naked. And then, beg all you want; you won't get a single vote. Your days are numbered. We'll drag you through the gutter. That is a promise!

Both Arjun and he stalk out in a huff...

Balram is obviously pleased with his achievement...

ARJUN
अरे !...

BALRAM SINGH
अरे!...

ARJUN
ख़बरदार जो एक शब्द बोला दादूजी के बारे में तो!...

BALRAM SINGH *(Cool as a cucumber)*
देखिए... देखिए...

KALIKANT
देखिए, देखिए.. ऐसी गर्मागर्मी...

BALRAM SINGH
देखिए... देखिए... सत्याग्रह का Violence!

ARJUN
अरे तेरी तो... अब्भी दिखाते हैं तेरे को Violence...

BALRAM SINGH
Distance पहलवान जी... आपको जेतना Up-down करना है कर लीजिए... मगर इस गठबंधन की सरकार में... हमारी मर्ज़ी के बग़ैर कोई कानून नहीं बनेगा... Understood!...

MANAV
कानून तो बनेगा बलराम सिंह... क्यूँकि आप जैसे Criminal Politicians को आज का नौजवान अच्छी तरह पहचान गया है... और गठबंधन तो क्या... आपकी भी गाँठ खोल कर ऐसा नंगा करेंगे... कि आप भीख माँगेंगे... और Vote का एक टुकड़ा भी नहीं मिलेगा... अपनी साँसें गिननी शुरू कर दीजिए मंत्री जी... खींच–खींच कर Gutter तक ले जाएँगे हम लोग... And thats a promise...

BALRAM SINGH

Sir! Sir!! Nice lecture! But in the legislative assembly, I am heard, not you.

BALRAM SINGH

अरे Sir...Sir.. अच्छा भाषण दिया आपने... लेकिन क्या है कि विधान सभा में Hearing हमारी होती है... आपकी नहीं...

SECRETARIAT -EXT - AFTERNOON

Manav and Arjun coming out-

ARJUN

Impotent, each one of them.

ARJUN

नपुंसक हैं सब के सब...

MANAV

Be that as it may, we can't lose uncle in their politics. No matter how, we'll have to get him to end his fast.

MANAV

जो भी हो, इनकी राजनीति में हम बाबूजी की जान गँवा नहीं सकते... जैसे भी हो... उनका अनशन तुड़वाना ही पड़ेगा...

RAMLEELA GROUND -EXT - AFTERNOON

Manav takes the microphone.

MANAV

It is obvious that the government will not comply with our demands.

MANAV

ये बात साफ़ है कि... सरकार हमारे निर्देशों का पालन नहीं करना चाहती...

PEOPLE

Long live...

PEOPLE

दादूजी जिंदाबाद...

MANAV

Perhaps they don't care about Daduji. But we do.
(The crowd falls silent)
I propose that Daduji break his fast. We will figure out another way to pressurize them. Our movement will..

MANAV

उन्हें शायद... दादू जी की जान की परवाह नहीं... लेकिन हमें उनकी चिंता है...
(The crowd falls silent)
मैं आप सब की तरफ़ से एक प्रस्ताव रखना चाहता हूँ... कि दादू जी अपना अनशन तोड़ दें... हम सब कुछ नये तरीके से सोचकर... सरकार पर दबाव डालेंगे... और इस आन्द –

PEOPLE

Daduji... Long live...

PEOPLE

दादूजी जिंदाबाद...

He turns around to find Dwarka standing behind him.. Dwarka steps forward..

DWARKA

I am grateful to you all... Your concern, your love and faith will lead us to our goal. But, now we cannot step back. I will continue my indefinite fast. I am within you all... and you all are within me. I will be lucky if I die for this cause.

DWARKA

आभारी हूँ मैं... आप लोगों की... चिंता के लिए... आपका प्यार... और विश्वास... हमें... हमारे Mission तक पहुँचाएगा... लेकिन... अब... हम... पीछे नहीं हट सकते... मेरा... अनशन... आमरण चलेगा... आप सब के अंदर... मैं हूँ... और... मुझमें आप सब... भाग्यशाली होउँगा मैं... यदि इस कारण... मेरी मृत्यु ही क्यों ना हो जाये... मेरी... मृत्यु ही क्यों ना हो जाये...

Arjun raises the slogan.

The fireman

The scene where a Satyagrahi sets himself on fire was tricky. But the young stuntman bravely set himself on fire and ran through the thick crowd taking special care not to go too close to anyone else. After the shot, the crew, cast and the entire crowd gave him an enthusiastic round of applause.

ARJUN
Long live Daduji.

ARJUN
दादू जी... अमर रहें...

PUBLIC
Long live..

PUBLIC
अमर रहें... अमर रहें...

In a sudden burst of frenzy, a young man runs through the crowd spilling a Canister of Kerosene on himself and screaming...

LALBAHADUR
Daduji, this government won't give us anything. We will die, but they won't care! Daduji, they don't care for us. Long live Daduji!

LALBAHADUR
दादूजी... ये सरकार हमें कुछ नहीं देने वाली... हम मर जायेंगे... खप जायेंगे... इन्हें हम लोगों की कोई परवाह नहीं है... दादूजी... दादूजी... जिन्दाबाद...

He reaches right up to the front of stage and before anyone can stop him, he sets himself on fire.

ARJUN
Hey...

ARJUN
ए!...

DWARKA
Stop him!

DWARKA
अरे इसको...

Manav and Arjun jump down from the stage pulling the stage cloth. They try to douse the fire but the man runs through the crowd like a running inferno. He finally collapses and they douse the fire-

MANAV
Call an Ambulance!

MANAV
Ambulance बुलाओ...

LALBAHADUR
Manav! Daduji has done so much for us, that I can even give my life.

LALBAHADUR
मानव भैया... दादूजी ने... हमारे लिये इतना किया... तो हम अपनी जान नहीं दे सकते क्या...

DWARKA
Oh God.

DWARKA
हे राम... हे राम...

An ambulance arrives. Manav looks stunned.

HOSPITAL CORRIDOR – EXT: DAY

As Manav sits devastated in the Hospital Corridor Arjun comes up to him -

ARJUN
His name was Lalbahadur.

ARJUN
लाल बहादुर नाम था उसका...

Outside, a huge crowd has gathered, including the media –

ARJUN
The people want a public funeral procession.

ARJUN
Public चाहती है कि उसकी शवयात्रा निकाली जाये...

The City S.P. present at the Hospital says –

CITY S.P.
See, without government's approval I cannot permit this.

CITY S.P.
देखिए, सरकार से बात किए बिना... हम इसकी Permission नहीं दे सकते...

The crowd shouts slogans.

CROWD
Long live Lal Bahadur!

CROWD
लाल बहादुर... अमर रहे...

Manav stands before them and raises his hand –

The public quietens down...

MANAV
He was very brave. We will have a public procession..

MANAV
बहुत बहादुर था वो... लाल बहादुर... उसकी शवयात्रा निकलेगी –

The City S.P. looks stunned.

RAMLEELA GROUND – BACK STAGE: EXT. DAY

Yasmin looks aghast. She confronts Manav and Arjun.

CROWD
Long live... Lalbahadur!...

CROWD
अमर रहे... अमर रहे... लाल बहादुर... अमर रहे...

YASMIN
How could you even think of allowing this! Lalbahadur did this in a fit of passion, but by calling him a martyr, we will encourage such a mentality. This is a very dangerous step.

YASMIN
ऐसा सोच भी कैसे सकते हो तुम... लाल बहादुर जुनून में एक हादसा कर बैठा लेकिन उसकी शहीदी यात्रा निकालना इस तरह की मानसिकता को और भी हवा देना होगा... बहुत ही ख़तरनाक कदम होगा ये...

MANAV
You aren't reading the public mood. People are furious. This is how they'll make the government react.

MANAV
तुम समय की सुई को पढ़ नहीं रही हो यास्मिन... जनता का गुस्सा उबल रहा है आज... अब वो इसी तरह सरकार तक अपनी बात पहुँचाएगी...

ARJUN
Yasmin, the decision was the people's. You believe in democracy, right? Conduct a poll of these thousands here.

ARJUN
यास्मिन, शहीदी यात्रा निकालने का फ़ैसला जनता का है... तुम तो लोकतंत्र में विश्वास करती हो ना... देखो... हज़ारों जमा हैं यहाँ... अभी चलो और कर लो Voting...

Yasmin is shaking her head –

YASMIN
Democracy doesn't mean mob's vote, Arjun.

YASMIN
भीड़ के Vote से लोकतंत्र नहीं बनता अर्जुन...

YASMIN
Fine. I propose that we take the opinion of our entire committee.

YASMIN
ठीक है... मेरा प्रस्ताव है इस बात पर हमें जन–सत्याग्रह के सभी सदस्यों की राय लेनी चाहिए...

Manav comes up to her –

MANAV
Their opinion is here, before you.

MANAV
सभी की राय तुम्हारे सामने है...

Yasmin looks pained as she looks at him –

YASMIN
No, Manav. We don't have Daduji's opinion yet.

YASMIN
नहीं, मानव... दादू जी की राय अभी बाकी है...

MANAV
I don't consider it appropriate to disturb him in his state.

MANAV
बाबूजी को इस हालत में परेशान करना... मैं मुनासिब नहीं समझता...

It is a final statement. A challenge. Yasmin looks at him, he stares back. Face off.

YASMIN
I guess this was inevitable. It's been obvious for a while now that your views and decisions are assumed to be the committee's opinion. But today I want to register my opposition, even if I am alone.

YASMIN
I guess... ये तो होना ही था... कुछ दिनों से ज़ाहिर है कि तुम्हारी सोच और Decisions समिति की राय मान ली जाती है... लेकिन, आज मैं अपनी ख़िलाफ़त दर्ज़ करना चाहती हूँ... चाहे मैं अकेली क्यों ना हूँ...

She walks upto Manav and whispers –

YASMIN
Congratulations! I pray that you don't ever have to regret this decision of yours.

YASMIN
मुबारक हो... अल्लाह से दुआ करूँगी तुम्हारे इस फ़ैसले पे कभी अफ़सोस न करना पड़े...

RAMLEELA GROUND – BACK STAGE: EXT. DAY

Arjun walks up to a distraught Manav, sympathetically putting his hand on his shoulder..

MANAV
Why can't she understand? People are shaken up. If they come out on the streets, it will bring public pressure on the government. Else, Uncle's fast will...

MANAV
समझती क्यूँ नहीं यास्मिन??... लोग बौखला गये हैं... सड़कों पर निकलेंगे तो Public का Pressure पड़ेगा सरकार पर... वर्ना बाउजी का अनशन तो...

Shakes his head...

CITY STREET/ GANDHI CHOWK: EXT. DAY

The procession led by Arjun, Manav and other Core-Committee members passes the Gandhi Chowk peacefully. There are 3-4 Cops walking at the end of the procession.

MAN-1
You bloody government dog!

MAN-1
स्साले ख़ाकी वर्दी वाले सरकारी कुत्ते...

The Cops ignore the remark..

MAN-2
They're behaving like it's a wedding party.

MAN-2
ऐसे चल रहे हो जैसे Party और बारात में आये हैं...

Another one walks right upto them and speaks into their face.

G.S.PARTY MAN
He's here to dance at a Martyr's mourning.

G.S.PARTY MAN
शहीद के जनाजे पर... Dance करने आया स्साला...

The cop pushes him out of the way.

COP
Take it easy! We're on duty here.

COP
ए... तमीज़ से बात कर... Duty कर रहे हैं हम लोग...

Man One laughs..

MAN-1
Yeah right! Duty, indeed! Slimy bloody cop!

MAN-1
ये देखो... Duty कर रहा है... पुलिसवाला लुच्चा स्साला...

The Cop gets angered and hits the man with his stick.

COP
You..!!

COP
ए... तेरी तो -

Suddenly, several people jump on the Cops.People in the market all gather and begin to beat up the Cops. They pull and drag their bodies right upto the main chowk.

Manav and Arjun having got wind of this incident come running, concern written large on their faces.

CABINET HALL: DAY

Balram Singh walks up to the Chief Minister –

BALRAM SINGH
Enough is enough, Chief Minister! I had asked you not to allow this procession. Now, Ambikapur is burning. And, if I go down, I'll take you with me. I'm sending in the paramilitary! Sign it! Sign it!! Please!

BALRAM SINGH
Enough हो गया मुख्यमंत्री जी... Enough... मैंने पहले ही Warn किया था कि ये शव यात्रा ना होने दो!... अब अम्बिकापुर जल रहा है... अऽ हमारा भविष्य जल गया तो आप भी नहीं बच पायेंगे उसकी आँच से... मैं Para Military Force भेज रहा हूँ... Sign it... Sign it... Please...

GANDHI CHOWK: DAY

The city looks like a War Zone.... Sporadic riots-Vehicles burn– Everyone running to safety- Cops at Police stations guarding like armies under attack – Arjun runs on the street with his men, brandishing guns and other weapons.

ARJUN
Not behind me. Go block that way. And you there! You people come here! Don't let anyone in!

ARJUN
ए.. मेरे पीछे कहाँ सब... जाके Block करो उधर... Block कर वहाँ पर... तुम लोग इधर आओ... एऽऽ किसी को अंदर मत आने देना...

The S.P. with the paramilitary announces from outside the city walls-

CITY-S.P.
Police and CRPF are here to protect you. Don't take the law into your own hands, else we will deal with it firmly.

CITY-S.P.
पुलिस और C.R.P.F. आपकी रक्षा के लिए तैनात हैं... कानून अपने हाथ में मत लीजिए... वर्ना हम सख़्ती से पेश आएँगे...

GANDHI CHOWK – EXT: EXT. DAY

Just as Manav reaches Gandhi Chowk, Arjun and his men are running from one street to another.

MANAV
Gather your people. We need to control the situation.

MANAV
अर्जुन... सबको जमा करो... Situation को सँभालना होगा...

ARJUN
The situation is completely in our control, Manav. All the roads have been blocked. We won't let the CRPF or the police enter this city today. No matter what!

ARJUN
Situation पूरी तरह हमारे Control में है मानव... सारे रास्ते Block कर दिए हैं... इस शहर के अंदर C.R.P.F., Police किसी को आज घुसने नहीं देंगे... आज चाहे कुछ भी हो जाये...

MANAV *(agitated now)*
Arjun, violence is not our way! There'll be a lot of bloodshed!

MANAV *(agitated now)*
अर्जुन, हमारा रास्ता हिंसा और टकराव का नहीं है... बहुत ख़ून ख़राबा होगा...

ARJUN
So be it, Manav. What's left now? People are sick of this government. It's do or die today. We will show that bloody Balram Singh that we aren't cowards. Using the military against his own people!!

ARJUN
तो हो जाने दो मानव... अब बचा भी क्या है... तंग आ चुके हैं इस सरकार से... आज मर जायेंगे, लेकिन लड़ेंगे ज़रूर!... दिखा देंगे उस स्साले बलराम सिंह को कि हम कायर नहीं हैं... अपने ही लोगों पर Military चढ़ाता है...

MANAV
Don't be crazy, Arjun!! Daduji will never approve this movement becoming violent.

MANAV
पागल मत बनो, अर्जुन!!... दादूजी कभी नहीं चाहेंगे कि हमारा आंदोलन हिंसा –

ARJUN
You take care of Daduji, Manav! You do that!
(to his men)
Let's go!

ARJUN
दादूजी को तुम सम्हालो मानव... तुम सम्हालो...
(to his men)
चल ओए...

He joins his boys who are screaming –
It's this way or that way! Or else to the grave!

"अब की बार – आर या पार... कफ़न बाँध के – हैं तैयार!..."

Sumitra arrives looking terrified..

SUMITRA
Manav, please come fast. I don't know where Babuji has gone!

SUMITRA
मानव भैया... भइया जल्दी चलिये... बाबूजी पता नहीं कहाँ चले गये हैं...

MANAV
What do you mean?

MANAV
क्या मतलब?...

SUMITRA
I don't know.. No one saw him! Go find him! Please!!

SUMITRA
I don't know... किसी ने उन्हें नहीं देखा... पता नहीं कहाँ चले गये...

AMBIKAPUR STREETS: EXT. DAY

Manav begins to run in the streets.

Just as he turns, Yasmin's car appears. He stops her vehicle and comes to her window.

MANAV
Where are you going, Yasmin?

MANAV
कहाँ जा रही हो यास्मिन?...

YASMIN
I am leaving this town.

YASMIN
शहर छोड़ के जा रही हूँ...

MANAV
Please, Yasmin. Not now. I need you here.

MANAV
Please, Yasmin, अभी नहीं... I need you here!

Yasmin looks at him and shakes her head.

YASMIN
I can't help you, Manav.

YASMIN
मैं तुम्हारी मदद नहीं कर सकती मानव...

MANAV
I won't be able to stop this chaos without your help.

MANAV
तुम्हारी मदद के बिना मैं रोक नहीं पाउँगा इस Chaos को...

YASMIN
No one can stop it now, Manav. After all, everyone believes that it has your approval.

YASMIN
अब कोई नहीं रोक सकता मानव...हर कोई तो ये समझ रहा है कि तुम्हारी मंज़ूरी है इसको...

MANAV
This wasn't my intention, Yasmin! But I accept my mistake. Right now, we have an emergency. Uncle is missing.

MANAV
मेरा इरादा ये नहीं था, यास्मिन!... लेकिन फिर भी अपनी ग़लती मानता हूँ... इस वक़्त एक Emergency आ गयी है... बाउजी पता नहीं कहाँ चले गये!...

A shocked Yasmin steps out of her car..

YASMIN
Oh my God!

YASMIN
Oh my God!

MANAV
I'll look for him. You please try and convey to the people not to fight the police!

MANAV
मैं उनको ढूँढ़ता हूँ... तुम Please किसी तरह लोगों तक Message पहुँचाओ... कि वो पुलिस का सामना ना करें...

TOWN-STREETS: DAY

Dwarka, in a drowsy state, tries to stop a unit of armed forces from marching on. He encounters groups of people, brandishing arms to take position, and motions to them to maintain peace.

DWARKA
Stop!.. Stop!!.. What are you people doing? Stop!

DWARKA
अरे... रुकिये... अरे... रुकिये... कहाँ जा रहे हैं आप लोग... रुकिये... रुकिये... अरे... रुकिये... कहाँ... कहाँ जा रहे हैं... कहाँ जा रहे हैं आप लोग... रुक जाइए...

Bulbul speaks to Balram Singh on the phone.

BULBUL SINGH
Sir, Dwarka is right here.

BULBUL SINGH
Sir, द्वारका इधर ही है Sir...

BALRAM SINGH
Really?

BALRAM SINGH
अँयँ...

BULBUL SINGH
Give me the order Sir.

BULBUL SINGH
Order दीजिए Sir... Sir, Order...

BALRAM SINGH
Finish him!

BALRAM SINGH
Finish कर दे...

DWARKA
Stop!.. Stop!!..

DWARKA
रुक जाइए... रुक जाइए...

Manav races through the streets jumping over the barricades setup by the people. He encounters the CRPF outside and signals to say that he's not armed.

And then he spots Dwarka and runs towards him.

MANAV
Uncle...

MANAV
बाउजी....

DWARKA
Stop... Stop... No... No... No... Look here... Listen...

DWARKA
रुकिए... रुक जाइए... नहीं... नहीं... नहीं... नहीं... नहीं... देखिए... सुनिए...

MANAV
Uncle, Stop!..

MANAV
रुकिए बाउजी... बाउजीऽऽऽऽ....

BULBUL SINGH
Sir, I have both Dwarka and Manav in my sights.

BULBUL SINGH
Sir.. द्वारका और मानव... दोनों मेरे Gun Point पे हैं Sir..

BALRAM SINGH
Kill, kill, kill..

BALRAM SINGH
मार मार मार मार मार मार...

Dadu climbs some stairs to get to a vantage point.He waves his frail arms on both sides meaning them to keep calm.

DWARKA
No... Stop... Stop...

DWARKA
नहीं नहीं... रुक जाओ... देखो... रुक जाओ...

We notice Balram Singh's men taking a vantage position. Bulbul spots Manav running. Talks on phone with Balram Singh and fires.

Manav runs to save Dadu – He dives – Gets shot on his shoulder. A cross fire starts, with several bullets hitting Dwarka.

DWARKA
Manav...

DWARKA
मानव... मानव...

BULBUL *(on the phone to Balram Singh)*
I got both of them!

BULBUL *(on the phone to Balram Singh)*
दोनों को ठोक दिया...

TOWN-STREETS: EXT. DAY

Arjun, who had seen Bulbul and his men opening fire at Daadu chases him down.

Arjun snatches his phone and flashes it to the C.R.P.F. Commandant.

ARJUN
You son of a bitch!!

ARJUN
तेरी तो... पकड़ो साले को...

DURGALAL
Don't kill him!!!

DURGALAL
नहीं मारना नहीं...

ARJUN
Look, he was talking to the Home Minister.

ARJUN
ये देखो... Home Minister से बात कर रहा था... देखो..

TOWN-STREETS: EXT. DAY

The news spreads like wild fire and Yasmin has to push people out of the way before she reaches a dying Dwarka. Sumitra runs up to him.

SUMITRA
Father!

SUMITRA
बाबूजी...

YASMIN
Somebody call an ambulance!

YASMIN
Ambulance.. बुलाओ कोई...

SUMITRA
Father!

SUMITRA
बाबूजी...

Dwarka stops her.

Dwarka stops her.

DWARKA
No... it will be too late.

DWARKA
नहीं... नहीं देर हो जाएगी...

SUMITRA
Call a Doctor... Please, fast...

SUMITRA
भइया Doctor...जल्दी, Please जल्दी...

DWARKA *(Anguished and clearly in pain)*
Before word spreads... My message... Hurry up.

DWARKA *(Anguished and clearly in pain)*
इससे पहले कि ख़बर फैले... मेरा संदेश... मेरा संदेश... जल्दी करो...

DWARKA
I have very little time.

DWARKA
वक़्त... वक़्त बहुत कम है मेरे पास...

Yasmin's hands tremble as she sets up her Camera.

SUMITRA
Please, Father.

SUMITRA
Please, बाउजी...

He props himself on Manav's arm and begins to speak.

DWARKA
Stop this violence... Stop this violence... Or, I will die thinking that I made a mistake by starting this movement!

DWARKA
नहीं... इस... इस... इस हिंसा को... रोको!... रोको इस... हिंसा को... नहीं तो... जाते समय... मैं सोचूँगा... कि... इस आंदोलन को शुरू करके... मैंने ग़लती की...

Dadu's image and words are being watched by people huddled in groups all over the city.

Small T.V. sets being run on generators at Gandhi Chowk.

People look stunned as they watch and hear him.

DWARKA
What kind of nation have we made! Where leaders who run the government have disconnected from us. They refuse to even hear us out. What kind of nation have we made.. Peace..

DWARKA
येऽ... कैसा... देश... बनाया है हमने... कैसा देश... जहाँ सरकार... चलाने वाले लोग... कट गये हैं हमसे... हमारी... सुनने को तैयार ही नहीं वो... येऽ... कैसा... देश बनाया है हमने... शांति... शऽ!!!...

And, he dies..

ARJUN
Daduji...

ARJUN
दादूजी... दादूजी...

MANAV
Uncle...

MANAV
बाउजी...

SUMITRA
Father...

SUMITRA
भइया... बाबूजीऽऽऽ...

MANAV
Uncle...

MANAV
बाउजी...

His words, in a raspish echo, travel like waves through the crowds...
"What kind of a nation have we made?"

His words, in a raspish echo, travel like waves through the crowds...
'ये कैसा देश बनाया है हमने...'

CABINET COMMITTEE ROOM-INT: DAY

Kalikant Babu speaks to the DGP and senior officers, as a crestfallen C.M. turns away.

KALIKANT BABU
Arrest Balram Singh! And withdraw all the paramilitary forces from Ambikapur.

KALIKANT BABU
बलराम सिंह को Arrest कीजिए... और अम्बिकापुर से सारे Para Military Forces तुरंत Withdraw कीजिए...

DGP
Sir!

DGP
Sir!

CORRIDOR-INT: DAY

The S.P. walking down the Corridor. He is reporting to someone over the phone.

HQ-COP
He's disappeared, sir!

HQ-COP
Sir, वो फ़रार हो गया है...

S.P.
Seal his house!

S.P.
Seal कर दो उसका घर...

BALRAM SINGH'S RESIDENCE: EXT. DAY

Balram Singh's House being sealed by city officials.

BALRAM SINGH'S HIDEOUT - INT. DAY

In his hideout set in the deserted property Balram is devastated.

BALRAM SINGH
Zero...

BALRAM SINGH
Zero...

He flings the door open and finds Manav standing there. In his madness Balram Singh continues to speak.

BALRAM SINGH
Stop this!.. Someone...

BALRAM SINGH
ए... रोको भाई.... रोको...

He stops suddenly - Balram makes a dash – Manav holds him.

Balram tries to fight – Manav beats him up - Drags him to the entrance as Police arrives to take him.

COP
Stop, Please!..

COP
रुक जाइए... Please..

BALRAM SINGH'S HIDEOUT - EXT. DAY

Manav looks tense as he they take him away.

We hear a huge rush of crowds shouting slogans outside.

Out in the dilapidated courtyard of the building where Balram has been hiding, hundreds of people have gathered and are chanting.

PEOPLE
Blood for blood!

PEOPLE
ख़ून का बदला – ख़ून से...

Suddenly, a hand darts out and reaches to grab Balram - It is Arjun!

ARJUN
He's not going anywhere! Hand him over to us! We will do justice here! Now!!

S.P.
Move away from here! Stop! Stop!

ARJUN
If you don't hand over Balram Singh to us, Ambikapur will burn...

MANAV *(Screams)*
Arjun!...

ARJUN
Ambikapur will burn!

MANAV
Come to your senses, Arjun!

Arjun cuts him sharply..

ARJUN
I'm very much in my senses, Manav. He hurt the people. Now, they will punish him!

People shout.

PEOPLE
Blood for blood!

YOUNG MAN-01
Just leave it to us!

YOUNG MAN-02
We'll deal with this. And with the law and the government.

Again someone leads and they shout the slogan.

YOUNG MAN-03
Blood for blood!

Manav stands his ground.

MANAV
That'll be wrong! Against Daduji's principles.

YOUNG MAN – 4
We'll figure out this principles business later, Manav.

ARJUN
कहीं नहीं जायेगा ये... हमारे हवाले करो इसे... यहीं इन्साफ़ करेंगे... अभी!!!...

S.P.
हटिए यहाँ से... रुक जाइए... रुक जाइए...

ARJUN
अगर बलराम सिंह को हमारे हवाले नहीं किया तो आग लग जायेगी अम्बिकापुर में... जला कर रख देंगे सब कुछ...

MANAV *(Screams)*
अर्जुन!...

ARJUN
आग लग जाएगी अम्बिकापुर में...

MANAV
होश में आओ अर्जुन...

ARJUN
होश में हूँ, मानव... ये जनता का गुनहगार है... जनता ही सज़ा देगी इसे!...

PEOPLE
ख़ून का बदला ख़ून से...

YOUNG MAN-01
आप बस हट जाओ... हम पर छोड़ दो...

YOUNG MAN-02
सलट लेंगे हम... कानून से और सरकार से भी...

YOUNG MAN-03
ख़ून का बदला... ख़ून से...

MANAV
ये ग़लत होगा... दादूजी के सिद्धान्तों के ख़िलाफ़...

YOUNG MAN – 4
सिद्धान्तों की किताब हम बाद में पढ़ लेंगे मानव भैया...

MANAV

Shut up!!

Arjun comes to Manav and speaks persuasively.

ARJUN

Don't stop us today, Manav. If he escapes punishment, we'll regret forever.

Manav snaps!

MANAV

No, Arjun. I don't want us to repeat the same mistake that cost Daduji his life! It isn't that my blood isn't boiling.
(Pointing at Balram Singh)
I feel like tearing him limb from limb. But, that would be madness! The anger of us youth is entirely legitimate. We're this country's greatest strength and hope. And this anger has so much strength that if it transforms into a revolution, it can uproot the strongest system. Hence, don't waste this anger in revenge. Nurture it, and build your future!

Now, they listen intently..

MANAV *[contd.]*

Don't forget with what difficulty, giving up their own comfort, our parents educated us. Made us capable, so that we can make our future. But, if the country's future is in darkness, how can ours be bright? That's why we have to change politics. Arjun, not from outside, but by participating in it. With a group of young people, form a party on the principles of our movement. We'll all support you. Then let us see how the dividers and looters of this country continue their business! We'll keep Dadu alive! Amidst us! And, never let this flame die out!

MANAV

Shut up!!

ARJUN

आज मत रोको हमको मानव... अगर ये बच गया तो हमेशा अफ़सोस रहेगा...

MANAV

नहीं, अर्जुन... हमारी जिस ग़लती की वजह से दादूजी की जान गई... वो मैं दोबारा नहीं होने दूँगा... ऐसा नहीं है... कि मेरा ख़ून ठंडा पड़ गया है...
(Pointing at Balram Singh)
जी चाहता है कि इसके चीथड़े कर दूँ... लेकिन ये पागलपन होगा... पूरी तरह जायज़ है हम नौजवानों का गुस्सा... इस देश की सबसे बड़ी आबादी और उम्मीद हैं हम... और इस गुस्से में इतनी ताक़त है... कि अगर वो क्रांति में बदल जाये... तो बड़ी से बड़ी व्यवस्था को उखाड़ कर फेंक सकती है... इसीलिए अपने इस गुस्से को बदले की भावना में बर्बाद मत करो... उसे पाल कर रखो और अपना भविष्य बनाओ...

MANAV *[contd.]*

मत भूलो कि कितनी मुश्किलों से... अपना पेट काट कर... अपना सुख बेच कर हमारे माँ–बाप ने हमको पढ़ाया... क़ाबिल बनाया... ताकि हम अपना Future बना सकें... लेकिन जब तक देश का ही Future अंधकार में है... तो हमारा उज्जवल कैसे होगा?... इसीलिए हमें राजनीति को बदलना होगा... अर्जुन... बाहर से नहीं... बल्कि उनमें शामिल होकर... तुम Committed नौजवानों के साथ मिलकर जन सत्याग्रह के सिद्धान्तों पर Party बनाओ... हम सब समर्थन देंगे... फिर देखते हैं कि देश को लूटने वाले... बाँटने वाले कैसे चलाते है अपनी बेईमानी का बाज़ार!... हम दादू को जिन्दा रखेंगे... अपने बीच... और कभी इस आग़ को बुझने नहीं देंगे...

DWARKA HOUSE-INT: NIGHT

Manav comes to Dwarka's house and fondly looks at his portrait. His eyes well up.

GANDHI CHOWK-INT: NIGHT

Dadu's death brings complete gloom to the town. Gandhi's statue set against an evening sky- The mosque in the background - Candles lit all over the platform and the floor - Large portrait of Dadu's smiling face placed on the platform.

Thousands of people sit on the floor in silence.

A song plays in the background.

END CREDITS.

❊❊❊

Film Credits

UTV Motion Pictures Presents

Prakash Jha Productions'

SATYAGRAHA

A Prakash Jha Film

Our Special Thanks and Gratitude to the Late Mrs. Helen Wallia

Sincere Thanks

Manoj Shrivastava I.A.S., Pravin Garg I.A.S., S.K. Mishra I.A.S., Nikunj Srivastava I.A.S., Rajneesh Srivastava I.A.S., T. Srinivas Verma I.P.S., Nishant Barwadwe I.A.S., K.K. Singh I.A.S., Mohan Lal Meena I.A.S., Shashikant Shukla I.P.S., Vishesh Garhpale I.A.S., Pankaj Rag I.A.S., Sachin Sinha, I.A.S., Uma Shankar Bhargava

Anshuman Singh, Arvind Saxena, Ajay Pandey, Basant Kurre, Rajesh Chandel, Manu Vyas, Rajesh Mishra, Sunderlal Patel, Surendra Singh Senger, Kishore Kanal, R.K. Mehra, Umrao Singh Maravi, Narendra Babu Yadav, Rajendra Maliviya, Sunil Shrivastava, Chandramohan Mishra, Ravi Prakash Dhuni Bale, Rajagopal P.V., Aneesh Thillenkery, Sanjay Khande (E.E., PWD), A.A. Goury (S.D.O., PWD), Amit Singh

B.S.Yadav: I.E.S. Collage, Bhopal, Technocraft Institute of Technology (TIT), Jay Narayan Chaukasey (J.K. College & Hospital) Dr. Nirbhay Shrivastava, Dean, Gandhi Medical College, Rajkumar Pandey, P.S., Vidhan Sabha, Bhopal, Rajesh Upadhyay, D.E.O., Bhopal, Piyush Mathur, C.P.R.O., W.C.R., Jabalpur, Pranav Pradhan, Mukesh Hora, Vinod Shukla, Police Department, Bhopal/Raisen, Higher Education Department, Bhopal/Raisen, Press & Public Relation Dept., Bhopal/Raisen, Madhya Pradesh Tourism Development Corporation, Nagar Nigam Bhopal

Starring

Amitabh Bachchan, Ajay Devgn, Kareena Kapoor Khan, Arjun Rampal, Manoj Bajpayee, Amrita Rao, Indraneil Sengupta, Vinay Apte

Vipin Sharma, Manoj Kolhatkar, Shireesh Sharma, Ajay Trehan, Sahedev Gireesh, Raj Arjun Singh, Jagat Singh Solanki, Masood Akhtar, Pradeep Kukreja, Mitalee Jagtap, Vijay Gupta

Special Dance Performance: Natasa Stankovic

Special Appearance: Mugdha Godse

DI Colorist
Rob Lang

DI, VFX & Lab
Prasad Film Lab, Mumbai

Publicity Design
Studio Link Pvt. Ltd.

Publicity Stills
Chandan Kachhawa

Visual Promotions
Trigger Happy

Production Consultants, Bhopal
Zulfikar Ali
Zaid Ali

Steadicam Operator
Pranav Raval

Jimmy Jib Operator
Ameya Mahapatra

Associate Cinematographer
Aarup Mondal

Production Managers
Rishi Kumar Jha
Rajesh Kumar Khanna
Disha Jha

Chartered Accountant
Anil Sekhri & Co.

First Assistant Director
Iti Agarwal

Chief Assistant Director
Ritam Srivastava

Disney TV Marketing, Syndication & Distribution
Shikha Kapur
Amrita Pandey
Gaurav Verma
Lokesh Dhar
Prakash Nathan
Vishwas Joshi

Casting
Shruti Mahajan
Parag Mehta

Additional Casting
Ritam Srivastava

Mixing Engineer
Leslie Fernandes (Flavours Film Mix)

Choreography
Jayesh Pradhan
Uma–Gaiti ('Aiyo Ji')

General Manager (Prakash Jha Productions)
K.L. Chhabra

Creative Consultant
Alankrita Shrivastava

Production Controller
Sudhirbhai Mishra

Costumes
Priyanka Mundada

Art Director
Udai Prakash Singh

Action Director
Abbas Ali Moghul

Associate Director
Karan Talwar

Lyrics
Prasoon Joshi

Songs Composed by
Salim–Sulaiman ('Satyagraha', 'Aiyo Ji')
Aadesh Shrivastava ('Ras Ke Bhare')
Meet Bros Anjjan ('Janta Rocks')
Indian Ocean ('Hum Bhole The')

Music
Salim–Sulaiman

Audiography
Rakesh Ranjan

Editor
Santosh Mandal (A.F.E.)

Written by
Prakash Jha
Anjum Rajabali

Director of Photography
Sachin Krishn

Produced by
Prakash Jha
Ronnie Screwvala
Siddharth Roy Kapur

Directed by
Prakash Jha

Script Supervisor
Ram Goutam

Associate Screenplay Writer
Ravinder Randhawa

Key Assistant Directors
Lalit Jha, Palash Singh

Action Continuity
Kuldeep Yadav

2nd Assistant Directors
Tuhar Seth, Udit Jawarani

2nd 2nd Assistant Directors
Gauri Daswani, Suvrata Nasnodkar

Assistant Director: Art
Abhijit Gaonkar, Videeta Molasi

Associate Editor
Sundar Pathuri

Also Featuring
Mukul Chadda as Harinath
Sartaj Alam as Raghunath
Aarti Rautela as Nancy
Himanshu Gokani as H. Parekh
Ivan Rodriguez as Channel Head
Dishwa as ABP Anchor
Pooja Choudhary as Anchor 2
Anajani Kumar as Tuition Teacher
Nishit Broker as Sebi Spokesperson
Naveen Kaushik as Manav's Business Associate
Chetan Kapoor as ABP Reporter
Vikram Dahiya as Man On Fire

Focus Pullers
Gopal Avinash Malo, Dinesh Soni

Chief Assistant D.O.P.
Shrikant Asati

Assistant D.O.P.
Saurabh Kumar, S.K. Abdul Samad

Assistant Art Director
Ajeet Kumar, Sachin Dabade, Puranjay Singh Varma

Chief Costume Assistant
Gauri Navghare

Costume Assistant
Devyani Rode

Clap Boy
Jai Priyadarshi

Trainee Direction Assistants
Ashok Sen, Mahmood Khan, Saurabh Bharat, Gaurav Dubey, Swapnill Sharma, Rajiv Jha, Shruti Singh, Shrey Srivastava, Saksham Agarwal, Siddhant Sawant, Pushkar Ojha

Costume Assistants, Bhopal
Anvita Jain, Sara Chughtai, Richa Parashar, Shubham Gaikwad

Production Assistants
Harsh Mainra, Rishab Shrivastava, Archna Dosija, Jayesh Kumar, Rajneesh Jaiswal, Gopal K. Paswan, Rajesh Tiwari, Abhishek Srivastava, Nandan Jha, Rahul Kumar Tripathi

Head Spot
Moti Shah

Local Casting
Palash Singh, Lalit Jha

Artist Co-Coordinators, Bhopal
Avinash Dixit, Dilip Mosoom, Rohit Bhatnagar, Animesh Mehta, Hriday Sharma, Raj Bharti, Amit Sharma, Hesh Jain, Ramesh Kathane, Anjali, Krishna Patel, Sunil Raj, Ashraf Khan, Md Shafiq, Sudhir Ahirwar, Bhupendra Singh Rajput, Md. Salamuddin, Sachin Jain, Devesh Tiwary, Neeraj Piple, Sohail Khan, Dharmendra Parihar, Richin Srivastava, Zoaib Khan, Deepak Viswakarma

MARKETING AND PUBLICITY TEAM
Prakash Jha Productions
Iti Agarwal, Karan Talwar, Tushar Seth

DISNEY UTV TEAM
India Distribution Team
Praveen Trikha, A.Chandrasekaran, Naresh Bahukhandi, Deepak Upreti, Gobind Chawla, Vijay Giri, Dinesh K Badlani, Sajid Shaikh, Sumeet Singh, Sathish Kumar, Pradeep Tiwari, Francis Fernandes, Dhanesh Bhanushali, Rakhee Sharma, Bijay Kumar, Prashant Panicker, Hari Babu Anantha, Uday Arya, Veeramahendran Murugan, Nitin Sharma, Narayan Redkar, Nitin Verma, Vijay Mohan, Sukhbir Singh, Shailesh Lad, Sachin Chavan, Sartaj Alam, Ajay Giri, Ajay Jaswal, Adil Atik Ahmed, Jyotiram Thorat, Nitin Jadav, Vijay Taral, Ashok Pelli, Ashwin Parmar, Amit Shukla, Dinesh More, Ram Vilas, Alex Pandioan

International Distribution & Syndication Team
Rishi Kaul, Sonakshi Adhikari, Hindavi Aware, Abigail Rodrigues, Neha Kaul, Sumita Kewalramani, Kaushik Dedhia, Puja Tshering, Richa Dhar, Darshan Bhanushali, Mohijit Mukerjee, Jatin Talwar, Prakash Chandran, Vinitha Vinayachandran, Mamta Kamtikar, Kanan Dave, Ritu Madhotra, Mayur Vyas

Marketing Team
Raul Sin, Yogesh Satam, Rohit Kulkarni, Prithwish Ganguly, Ashley Lobo, Pashan Jal, Amanpreet Singh, Ankur Sualy, Yash Suchak, Punit Dawda, Tamagna Ghosh, Laalit Lobo, Aanchal Maheswari, Jimit Kansara, Bhavin Mehta, Hemanshu Mistry, Shruti Sundaraman, Pooja Nikam, Gurcharan Kaur

Research Team
Monika Yadav, Priyankar Basu

Operations Team
Prem N. Shetty, Naimish Shah, Menino Barretto, Megha Dabi, Krishnan Sainath, Anand Muppanar, Dharmesh Morthania, Dhaval Thaker, Sunayna Jaya Amin, Vinayak Chikane

Corporate Communications Team
Jyotika Ahuja, Sujata Chanda, Manisha Sharma

Legal Team
Naina Chhugani, Rohini Boez, Niranjana Unnikrishnan, Vishal Narichania, Ashutosh Pandey, Jidnyasa Vartak, Raashi Ahluwalia, Pritam Patole

Finance Team
Bhushan Kapadia, Shrinivas V. Margam, Keyursinh Parmar, Hiren A. Nanavati, Ankit Raipuria, Sadanand Kadam, Sandanathi S., Prashant Barthwal, Mahesh Pawar, Sanjay Thasal, Ramanand Kunder, Paresh Dere, Rahul Mahamunkar

Coordinators
Clara Fernandez, Vimal Nirmal

Support Staff
Jeelani Shaikh, Sachin Sunder Jadhav, Anil Gambre, Vishal Vasant Sawant, Sudhesh Mohite, Sanjay Kadam, Sachin S. Tawade, Prabhakar Dawal, Mangesh Sawant, Prakash Sawant, Mahesh Gurav, Vishal Gurav

Studio Link Pvt. Ltd.
Atmanand Golatkar, Unnati Vivek Shinde, Vijay Jani

In – Film Graphic Design
Harsh Raman Singh Paul, Udit Jawarani, Karan Talwar

Sound Designing Team
Rahul Badwelkar, Rakshit Thantry

On Location Sound Recordist
Basant Kumar Singh

Assistant Sound Recordist
M.K. Singh, Santosh R. Singh

Sound Attendant
Rajesh, Hira Singh, Khaniya, Sumit

Walky Talky Attendant
Santosh Singh Jagga

Ambient Sound Recordist
Rahul Badwelkar

THE MAKING OF *SATYAGRAHA*

Making Director
Soheb Hasan

Assistant
Jehanne Jodie Fernandes

Editor
Sunil Gorule and Dinesh Naik

Subtitles
Fresh Television Pvt. Ltd., Nideesh Vaasu, Sunil F. Lewis, Parisha Gandhi, Maitrayee Avachat, Ravindra Jadhav

Head, Make-up Department
Ravi Futane

Make-up Assistants
Ajay Pawar, Amit Gupta

Hair
Mangala Sirsat

Accounts
Sunil Sawant, Vaibhav Morya, Manish Parab, Pragnya Rawt

Office Staff
Mohan Sarambalkar, Kailash Paswan, Abhay Verma, Abhishek Paswan, Amrendra Kumar, Santosh Mahto, Mahendra Mandal, Dayaram Yadav, Anil Jadav, Ramesh Yadav

DI, VFX, Lab & Camera Rentals
Prasad Film Labs Mumbai Pvt. Ltd., EFX – Magic In Motion

Executive Director
J. Naidu

Head of Operation
R. Shanker, Digital Intermediate Team

Colorist
Rob Lang

DI Executive Producer
Mangesh K. Bhalerao

DI Producer
Arvind Singh

DI Editorial Head
Venkat Naraharisetty

DI Editorial Team
Ganapathy Subramanian, Somasundaram Krishan, Kumar Selvaraj J., Muthuraj Ranalingam, Rajesh Yadav, Milind Kamblae, Chetan Gaikwad

Data Lab & Mastering Services
Amol Khanvilkar, Balram Modem, Mahesh Palyekar

Assistant – DMS
Sujit Das, Ganesh Prajapati, Dilip Chodankar

DI Online Team
Swapnil Vaishnav, Gopal B. Ray

Data Management
Pravin Shinde, Mayur Gaikwad, Hemanth Jhadav

Domain Specialist
Sony Antony

Neg Scanning & Recording Exec.
Pradeep Yadav

Neg Recording
Rajesh Yadav

Neg Scanning Team
Ganesh Shyam Gholap, Sanoj Vishwakarma, Manoj Lakkakula

Storage Specialist
Arun Kumar

Tech & Support Team
Raghu Rangnathan, Boopathy Thangamuthu, Surendra Nade, Basker R., Rhishikesh Zarapkar, Prathamesh Sawant

Technologist
Mithun D'souza, Sales & Key Accounts Team

V.P. Business Dev
Rajiv Ghosh

Assistant Managers
Gurupratap Singh, Madhulika Bansal

EFX – MAGIC IN MOTION

VISUAL EFFECTS TEAM, MUMBAI

Sr. VFX Supervisor
P. Mohan

Sr. Compositor
Mohamed Ghouse

Compositors
N. Naveen Kumar, G. Keerthivasan, Thiyagarajan C Mudaliyar, Swapnil Kulkarni

Jr. Compositors
Sanil Tendle, Gurpreet Singh Dhanjal, Mohan Raut, Kapil Prajapati

Paint Artist
Swapnil Hirave

Roto & Cleanup
Sanjay Dhanawade

Matte Painter
S. Satheesh

Motion Graphics
Nilesh Shinde

3D Generalist
Miraj Biswal

3D Lighting Artist
Kishore Shetty

Animator
A. Srinivasan

FX Artist
S. Arun Kumar

VISUAL EFFECTS TEAM, CHENNAI

Vice President – Prod. (VFX & DI)
K.Himakumar

Creative Head
G.Villavan Kothai

2D Head
V. Satheesh

3D Head
J.Ganeshan

Compositing Head
V. Sathyanarayana

Roto & Touch Up Head
C. Manimaran

Team Leader
Venkaatesh. B.R.

Project Co-Ordinator
Ramkumar S.

Compositing Team
Rethinakumar T., Hemadhri N., Koteeswaran.B.T., Sundar K., Panjabakesan, Annamalai K., Dinesh, Rekapalli Satish, Stalin, Karthik C., Shijil, Karthik D., Vijayakumar, Narendrababu, Savarinathan, Saravanan D., Suresh A., Baleshwar, Ravi Perumal, Arokiaraj, Chandravenu Keerthinathan, Prakash N.

3D Team
Raja Pandian H., Lokeshwaran P.K.

Paint & Roto Team
Sankar D.V., Mugilan A., Obli Chendrayan T., Magesh Kumar S., Sitharthan T., Deva Rajan M., Durairaj A., Balaji D., Mathi R., Navin Selva J., Veerapandian D., Anandan, Sivaraj S., Anand, Rajkumar R., Raja V., Srimurali, Selvarasu S.

Matte Paint Team
Gunasekaran M., Gurumoorthy D., G. Ganapathi Arumugam, Jayapraksah Narayanan.P

Camera Team
Prasad Panavision

HOD – Camera Rentals
Yogesh Anand

Executive Operations
Ornellas Saldhana, Jivan Mhatre

Technical & Prep Support
Peter McArthur, Ajey Kodlikeri, Nilesh Adwankar, Subil Mudaliar, Nilesh Ghonge

Back Office Support
Sanjay Chawan, Pravin Katkar, Sairam, Ashwini, Jagadish Abhang, Deepak Sakalp

Camera Attendant
Sunil Yadav, Aamir Sheikh, Raju Gupta, Shaikh Latifur Raheman, Mond. Hanif Shaikh

Dwarka Slap Animation
Pradeep Nayak

Dubbing Engineer
Sunil Sinha (Dhwani Recording Studio), Sanjay Survey (B.R. Studios)

Sound Editor
Shankar Singh

Dub – Matching & Stock Effects
Shankar Singh, Kailash Singh

Foley Effects
Mohammed Iqbal

Re-recording at
Flavours Film Mix

Assistant Mix Engineer
Joe Rodrigues, Souvik Phukan, Kingshuk Moran, Yogesh Nehe

Studio Manager
Domnic Godinho

Voice Coordinator
Champa Tiwari

Dubbing Artists
Shahnawaz Pradhan, Sanjeev Tiwari, Ankit Varshneya

Rakesh Vidua
Manoj Pandey, Vishal Kumar

Jasbeer Jassi
Riddhi Bansal, Neha Gargava

Krishna Rana
Nandini Sharma, Balvinder Kaur

Jeet Singh
Jay Prakash, Pallavi Jadhav

Amarjeet Singh
Mohit Sinha, Kuldeep Kaur, Background Music

Additional Programming
Abhijit Vaghani, Tanuj Tiku, Prasad Sashte, Raj Pandit, Pramod Timilsina

Copywriter and Score Editor
Pramod Timilsina

Guitars
Kalyan Baruah, Pramod Timilsina

Strings
Bombay Strings Orchestra

Cello
B.S. Srinivasan

Chorus
Rajiv Sundaresan, Hrishikesh Karmekar, François, Marianne D'Cruz, Neisha Mascarhennas.

Flute
Paras Nath

Vocals
Salim Merchant, Benny Dayal, Raj Pandit

Recorded at Blue Productions by
Aftab Khan, Pramod Timilsina, Raj Pandit

Strings Recorded at Aslam's Studio by
Aslam Khan & Benvin Fernandes

Mixed by
Aftab Khan at Blue Productions

Steady Cam Assistants
Abul Khan, Ram Mallah

Jimmy Jib Assistants
Rajesh Pawar, Imtiaz Khan, Nitesh Kukumati, Kishor Sahoo

Camera Attendants
Vijay Kotian, Mustak Shaikh, Anil T. Pardeshi, Yacin Tamboli

ACTION DEPARTMENT

Assistants
Murtuza Ali Moghul, Vikram Dahiya, Ashraf Khan

Stunt Men
Baquar Mirza, Irfan Yunus, Afzal Khan, Lakhwinder Sandhu, Rajendar Dahiya, Abid, Gregory D'Souza, Laxman, Deepak Sharma, Zoheb Noora, Umar Bala Lalit Mishra, Lala Latif, Mehmood Moghul, Aamir

Choreography Assistants
Jayesh Pradhan, Rutul Pancholi, Deepika Shetty, Sumona Chakravarthy, Uma–Gaiti

Choreography Assistants
Bob, Karishma Chavan

LOCATIONS: BHOPAL

Bhopal Municipal Cooperation, Janganana Bhavan, Mr. Hora's Bungalow, IES College of Engineering & Technology, J.K. College and Hospital, Noor-Us-Sabah Palace

Trinity Institute Of Technology, Central Library Grounds, Berkheri Village, Benezir College Ground, Mr. Pradhan's Bungalow, Bisenkheri Village

LOCATIONS: MUMBAI

Motilal Oswal Financial Services Ltd.
F Bar-One, India Bulls Center,
Empress Digital Studio

HOTELS: BHOPAL, M.P.

Noor-Us-Sabah Palace, Hotel Satya Villas, Hotel Surendra Landmark, Jehan Numa Palace, Hotel Amar Vilas, Hotel Shagun, Hotel Surendra Vilas, Hotel Neena Palace, Hotel Om Plaza

Censor Agent
Ravinder Singh

ART DEPARTMENT

Mistry
Narayan Singh

Head Carpenter
Ram Sevak Sharma

Painting Head
L.R. Mallah, Devnath Sahani, Rakesh Sahani

Setting Boys
Surendra Tiwari, Pankaj Singh, Anil Tiwari, Sabbir Khan, Ramesh Singh, Narendra Tiwari

DRESS DEPARTMENT
Umesh Kumar Pandey (Head), Shashikant Sharma, Satish Yadav,Sachin Pardeshi, Om Prakash Kanojia, Rajkumar Maurya, Alak Mandal, Rajesh Pillai, Yuvraj Paswan, Nadir Khan

Laundry
Babulal Pardeshi, Suresh Kanojia

LIGHTS AND CRANE ATTENDANTS

Gaffer
Ramakesh Yadav

Spark Light Man
Suryakant Barik, Wasim, Tapas, Ajay, Mohd Shamim, Sajid, Israr, Mohd Kalim, Munna Yadav, Shyam Yadav, Shiva, Jeevan, Mh Kumar Gowda, Faroque, Ashok, Khadanand Gautam, Mujib, Kamal Da, Ali, Azaam, Sohaib, Satendra Kumar Singh, Jabaar, Mohd Sarfaraz Alam, Ashish, Gopal, Rehaan, Ajju, Shanubaj, Munna Chaudhary, Vicky, Ramesh

Balloon Light–Balloon Operator
Imran Shaikh, Raju Gawda, Madan, Kumar K., Anand Panday, Dhamendar, Sandosh

Additional Light Boys
Chandrakant N. Anmanu, Chandru C.N., Gautam Sahu, Bandari Kumar Swamy, Om Prakash, Shabbir, Mobin Shaikh

Gun Attendant–Gun Master
Mukesh Kumar Singh
Assistants
Gopal Thakur, Bhanwar Singh, Viraj Kushwaha, Govind Kothari, Ashlam Khan

Security
Ace Security

ARTISTS' STAFF

AMITABH BACHCHAN

Manager
Rosy Singh, Praveen Jain

Hair and Make-up
Deepak Sawant

Bodyguard
Ravendra Ray, Ganesh Thevar, Kashinath Kargutkar, Jitendra Sinde

Asst. Making
Ankush Parekh

AJAY DEVGAN

Manager
Abhinav Singh

Make-up
Harish Wadhone

Hair
Jaipal Raskar

Boy
Lakhnath Basyal (Lekhu)

Trainer
Rohan Sawant

Guard
Pardeep Gautam

Cook
Narendra Singh Bisht

Driver
Tilak Saru

Masseuse
Chotu (Bhupraj Bassyal)

Vanity
Jeevan

KAREENA KAPOOR KHAN

Manager
Poonam Damania

Hair
Purshotam Hans

Make-up
Ritesh Naik

Boy
Bed Prakash Khanal

Trainer
Rekha Kalara

ARJUN RAMPAL

Manager
Chantelle Cabral

Make-up
Rajan Yaadav

Hair
Shivcharan Laxman Geloth, Nitin Gawli - Hakim Aalim

Staff
Tauheed Raja Ahmed

Trainer
Ivan Fernandes

MANOJ BAJPAYEE

Manager
H.N. Tripathi

Make-up
Milind Chavan

Hair
Hamid Shaikh

Boy
Aashish Patil
Amrita Rao

Manager
Aehuti Mistry

Manager
Ragini

Hair
Aruna More

Make-up
Vikram Kshetri

Boy
Uttam Ghosh

MUGHDA GODSE

Make-up
Mukesh Patil

Hair
Reena Palav

Spot
Ashok Kumbhar

NATASA STANKOVIC AS DANCER

Managed by
Toabh Talent Management

Hair
Mangla Sirsat

Make-up
Vani Nath

Auditors
Anil Sekhri & Co., Bhushan Kerkar Kishore Dabhelkar

Avid Technical Support
Prasanna K, Brunda Kumar, Nayan Shinde, Prerak Mehta, Varun Singh, Dilawar W. Desai

Production Boys
Moti Shah, Arvind Singh, Prashant Saraf, Pappu Shah, Ranjit Mandal, Din Mohd, Lallan Shah, Pankaj Panchal, Ganesh Yadav, Niranjan Singh, Govind Parihar, Indradev Paswan, Rana Pratap Singh, Chotu Prasad, Manoj Chourasia, Gorakh Kedre, Ajay Kamat

Catering
A.K. Caterers, Rasoi Magic Caterers

Suppliers

Light N Light, Welcome Store, Gem Dress, Prasad Lab: Camera Hire, Vision Plus – Steady Cam, Dream Eyes, Singh Sound, Welcome Stores Food Supplies, Krishna Glamour Stores, Durga Enterprises, Natural Hair, Ply Palace, Jigna Enterprises Generators, Prasad Labs Print & Processing, Gulshan Saw Mills, Magic Moves Cinequip, Kodak India Raw Stock, Light Craft, Jimmy Jib Mumba Devi Vanity Vans, Sing & Swing Rehearsal Hall, Meghdoot Traders, Reliable Audio Visual Rental
Action Plus, Ashok Sunita Chedella Co., Sai Video Broadcasting, Action Media Effect, Tarangs, R.K. Sound System, Thriller Special Effect, Manoj Purbey Props Supplier, New Sehgal Generators, Patel Dresswaala, Jal Dhara Water Suppliers

Transport
Sam Enterprises, Thakur Transport, Star Carevans (Vanity Van), Ashish, Yadav Tempo Service, Singh Vanities, Tejal Ketan Rawal (Vanity Van)

Ticketing
Rainbow Enterprises, Super Travel Agency, Vijay Pathak (Train Ticketing)

SONGS

1. 'Satyagraha'

   Vocals
   Rajiv Sundaresan, Shivam Pathak, Shweta Pandit

   Additional Vocals
   Salim Merchant, Raj Pandit, Aneesh Sharma.

   Lyrics
   Prasoon Joshi

   Composed by
   Salim–Sulaiman

2. 'Aiyo Ji'

   Vocals
   Salim Merchant, Shradha Pandit

   Lyrics
   Prasoon Joshi

   Composed by
   Salim–Sulaiman

   Additional Programming On 'Aiyo Ji'
   Gaurav Raina, Raj Pandit

   Additional Programming On 'Satyagraha'
   Raj Pandit

   Chorus
   Rajiv Sundaresan, Hrishikesh Karmekar and Neuman Pinto

   Guitars
   Warren Mendonsa

   Songs 'Satyagraha' and 'Aiyo Ji' Composed, Arranged and Produced by
   Salim Merchant and Sulaiman Merchant.

   Songs 'Satyagraha' and 'Aiyo Ji' Mixed and Mastered by
   Aftab Khan at Blue Productions.

   Songs 'Satyagraha' and 'Aiyo Ji' Recorded by
   Aftab Khan, Pramod Timilsina & Raj Pandit at Blue Productions.

3. 'Raske Bhare Tore Naina'

   Vocals
   Shafqat Amanat Ali and Arpita Chakraborty

   Lyrics
   Prasoon Joshi

   Composed by
   Aadesh Shrivastava

   Arranged by
   Amar Makwana

   Programmed by
   Sandeep Chatterjee

   Recorded at
   Studio A.V. Sound Mumbai & Beat Factory New Delhi

   Mixed and Mastered by
   Shaitus Joseph

4. 'Raske Bhare Tore Naina' House Mix

   Vocals
   Aadesh Shrivastava and Arpita Chakraborty

   Lyrics
   Prasoon Joshi

   Composed by
   Aadesh Shrivastava

   Arranger/Programmer
   Sandeep Chatterjee

   Recorded at
   Studio A.V. Sound

   Mixed and Mastered by
   Shaitus Joseph

5. 'Janta Rocks'

   Vocals
   Meet Bros Anjjan Feat, Keerthi Sagathia, Papon, Shibani Kashyap, Shalmali Kholgade, VIP

   Lyrics
   Prasoon Joshi

   Composed by
   Meet Bros, Anjjan

   Rap & Mimicry
   VIP

   Cricket Commentary
   Sunil Grover

   Child Vocals
   Meghna S. Mishra & Minakshi Bargode

   Backing Vocals
   Thomson Andrews, Given Dias, Ryan Dias, Keshia Braganza

   Programmed by
   John Stewart

   Guitar
   Sanjay Joseph

   Recorded by
   Gautam Chakrabortty & Uddipan Sharma

   Recorded at
   Meet Bros Recording Studio

   Mixed at
   J.S. Workstation by P.A. Deepak

   Mastered at
   Lurssen Mastering by Reuben Cohen

   Music Managed by
   Suraj Kumar

6. 'Hum Bhole The'

   Vocals
   Rahul Ram, Amit Kilam, Himanshu Joshi

   Lyrics
   Prasoon Joshi

   Composed by
   Indian Ocean

Publishing Partner: Om Books International